Cary L. Cooper is Professor of Organizational Psychology in the Manchester School of Management at UMIST. He is the author of over 60 books, 300 scholarly articles in academic journals and the Editor of *Journal of Organizational Behavior*. He has appeared on a number of television programmes (for instance, Channel Four's 'How to Survive the Nine to Five'), and has written numerous articles for national and international newspapers.

Marilyn J. Davidson is Senior Lecturer in Organizational Psychology in the Manchester School of Management at UMIST. She is the author of 10 books, scores of academic articles and the Editor of the journal, *Women in Management*, review and abstracts. She has appeared on numerous television and radio programmes including 'This Morning' and 'Start the Week', and is a Fellow of the British Psychology Society.

By Cary L. Cooper:

Living With Stress
Mergers and Acquisitions: The Human Factor
Causes, Coping and Consequences of Stress at Work

By Marilyn J. Davidson:

Vulnerable Workers – Psychosocial and Legal Issues
Women and Information Technology
*Reach For the Top: A Woman's Guide to Success in Business
    and Management*

CARY L. COOPER
& MARILYN J. DAVIDSON

The Stress Survivors

Experiences of Successful Personalities

Grafton
An Imprint of HarperCollins*Publishers*

To Rachel, Beth, Laura, Sarah and Scott
To Graham, Fern and Lloyd
To all those stress survivors who shared
their experiences with us.

Grafton
An Imprint of HarperCollins*Publishers*
77–85 Fulham Palace Road,
Hammersmith, London W6 8JB

A Grafton Original 1991
9 8 7 6 5 4 3 2 1

A catalogue record for this book
is available from the British Library

ISBN 0 586 21438 0

Set in Times

Printed in Great Britain by
HarperCollinsManufacturing Glasgow

Contents

1

Stress: the Black Plague of the Late Twentieth Century

'Stress', in our modern vocabularies, is used casually to describe a wide range of ills: 'She's under a lot of stress,' we say when trying to understand a friend's irritability or forgetfulness; 'It's a high-stress job,' someone says, awarding an odd sort of prestige to certain occupations; 'I'm really stressed out,' someone says to describe a vague yet often acute sense of fatigue or tiredness. But for those whose ability to cope with day-to-day matters is at a crisis point, the concept of stress is no longer a casual one; for them, 'stress' can mean 'illness'.

The purpose of this book is to explain the ways in which people cope with the pressures of their lives. We felt this could be more graphically illustrated by using 'achievers', well-known personalities who have experienced major 'crunch' events or pressures which tested their repertoire of coping strategies. What these personalities have in common is that they survived their crunch events, sometimes by coping effectively, and other times by failing to cope. It is hoped their experiences will help us to understand the processes of stress and coping.

In total, we carried out over a score of in-depth interviews with a cross-section of different personalities, whose 'notoriety' was a result of success in the world of the arts, media or business. The selection of these individuals was based both on our knowledge that they had reached the top of their respective professions, and survived the pressures, as well as their willingness to share their experiences openly with us. The following agreed to participate in our study: Pamela Armstrong (TV personality), Nina Carter (former international model and pop star), Sir Terence Conran (international designer and entrepreneur), Jonathan Dimbleby (TV and radio personality), David Emanuel (international dress designer and photographer), Elizabeth Emanuel (international dress designer and retailer), Judy Finnigan and Richard Madeley (co-hosts of the popular

This Morning TV programme), Joanna Foster (Chair of the Equal Opportunities Commission), Helen Fraser (senior UK publisher), Stuart Hall (TV and radio personality), Gloria Hunniford (TV and radio personality), Derek Jameson (journalist, TV and radio personality), Linda Kelsey (former editor of *Cosmopolitan* and current editor of *She* magazine), Victor Kiam (President of Remington Corporation and best-selling author), Roger McGough (poet, author and playwright), Austin Mitchell (Member of Parliament), Bel Mooney (author), Jonathan Powell (Controller of BBC1 TV), Eddie Shah (entrepreneur in the communications industry and founder of *Today* newspaper), Rick Wakeman (rock star) and Ann and Nicholas Winterton (Members of Parliament).

In these interviews, we asked them about their early childhood experiences, philosophy of life, 'crunch' points in their lives, their relationships at home, the stresses in their profession and, most importantly, how they managed to cope with a successful career and its accompanying pressures.

Our chosen approach of focusing on the individual and his or her attributes, as distinct from situational factors, helps us to understand what sort of people become leaders in their field and survive the pressures of success. Examining the attributes of leaders and successful copers has a long history. Plato described his 'philosopher king' as a rare individual possessing superior abilities as befits a 'man of gold'. In the *Republic*, he opens up the basic debate as to whether leaders or achievers in society are born or created, a debate which is still energetically carried on today. During the eighteenth and nineteenth centuries, many writers highlighted the importance of exploring the personal characteristics of individual leaders in a wide variety of arenas, something that has been referred to as the 'great man' approach (no sexual discrimination intended). Emerson in the US and Carlyle in England felt that the 'leading men' of their day, as in any other period of time, possessed special and unique talents which enabled them to achieve their position and success, while combating the pressures of life. Weber, writing at the end of the nineteenth century, identified the 'charismatic' as possessing qualities which help them overcome problems, resolve issues and lead by example.

Galton, in his book *Hereditary Genius* in 1869, demonstrated the linkages between persons of outstanding achievement in a variety of fields. He found that certain physical, intellectual, personality and coping techniques were common among distinguished leaders. Havelock Ellis in 1904 carried out the first empirical study of what he called the 'British Men of Genius!' He emphasized the balanced personalities and coping strategies of his subjects, 'who showed very little psychosis, although minor nervous disorders and poor health in childhood were rather frequent'. In 1926, Cox, in his book *The Early Mental Traits of Three Hundred Geniuses*, found that successful people in business, the arts and intellectual pursuits had two things in common, 'persistence' and 'drive'. And Tead in his 1935 book *The Art of Leadership* reported that the traits of the 'effective leader' were nervous and physical energy, a sense of purpose and direction, enthusiasm, friendliness, integrity, technical mastery, decisiveness, intelligence, teaching skills and faith. Barnard, in *The Function of the Executive* in 1948, stated that the significant traits that distinguished leaders from their followers were physique, determination, persistence, endurance and courage. Other writers and researchers have identified characteristics such as 'adjustment', 'good appearance', 'need for achievement', 'assertiveness' and 'fear of failure' as being necessary leadership and survival traits.

It is from this tradition that this book stems. We are not asking the question 'how do successful people differ from less than successful people?', as has been the case in much of the traditional 'great man' research, but rather 'what are the characteristics of individuals who have achieved success?', and 'how have they survived the stresses and strains of their job and lifestyle?'; in other words, what has been their recipe for dealing with the excessive demands of life? First, however, we must define what we mean by 'stress'.

What is Stress?

There is much disagreement over the definition of 'stress'. The term has been used to signify environmental agents which disturb structure and function, as well as responses to such agents in the different levels of psychological, physiological and sociological systems. Stress is a word derived from Latin, *stringere*, and was used popularly in the seventeenth century to mean *hardship*, *adversity* or *affliction*. During the late eighteenth century its use evolved to denote *force*, *pressure*, *strain* or *strong effort*, with reference primarily to a person or to a person's organs or mental powers.

Early definitions of strain and load used in physics and engineering eventually came to influence one concept of how stress affects individuals. Under this concept, external forces (load) are seen as exerting pressure upon an individual, producing strain. Proponents of this view indicate we can measure the stress to which an individual is subjected in the same way we can measure physical strain upon a machine.

The idea that stress contributes to long-term ill health (rather than merely short-term discomfort implicit in the above definition) can also be found early in the concept's development. In 1910, for example, Sir William Osler noted that angina pectoris was especially common among the Jewish members of the business community, and he attributed this, in part, to their hectic pace of life: 'Living an intense life, absorbed in his work, devoted to his pleasures, passionately devoted to his home, the nervous energy of the Jew is taxed to the uttermost, and his system is subjected to that stress and strain which seems to be a basic factor in so many cases of angina pectoris.'

The idea that environmental forces could actually cause disease rather than just short-term ill effects, and that people have a natural tendency to resist this, was seen in the work of Walter B. Cannon in the thirties. He studied the effects of stress upon animals and people, and in particular studied the 'fight or flight' reaction. Through this reaction, animals and people, when confronting extreme danger, will choose whether to stay and fight or try to escape. Dr Cannon observed that when his subjects experienced situations of cold, lack of oxygen and excitement, he could detect physiological changes such as emergency adrenalin secretions. Cannon described these individuals as being 'under stress'.

One of the first scientific attempts to explain the process of stress-related illness was made by physician and scholar Hans

Selye who in 1946 described three stages an individual encounters in stressful situations.

1. The *Alarm Reaction*, in which an initial phase of lowered resistance is followed by countershock, during which the individual's defence mechanisms become active.
2. *Resistance*, the stage of maximum adaptation and, it is hoped, successful return to equilibrium for the individual. If, however, the stressor continues or the defence does not work, he will move on to a third stage.
3. *Exhaustion*, when adaptive mechanisms collapse.

This theory reflected the prevalent feeling of the thirties and forties that stress could be understood exclusively by a simple stimulus-response model. Although many of the current definitions of stress still stick fairly closely to the stimulus-response or energy-exchange model of stress, there is a movement towards viewing it more as an *interactive process*. This more sophisticated viewpoint is particularly well articulated by the psychologist Richard Lazarus and marks the beginning of interactionist thinking. While pointing out that both the environmental stimulus and the reacting individual are vital elements, Lazarus emphasizes that it is the nature of the relationship between the two which is crucial: 'Stress refers, then, to a very broad class of problems differentiated from other problem areas because it deals with *any demands which tax the system*, whatever it is, a physiological system, a social system, or a psychological system, and the response of that system.' He goes on to say that the 'reaction depends on how the person interprets or appraises (consciously or unconsciously) the significance of a harmful, threatening or challenging event'.

By looking at stress as resulting from misfit between an individual and his or her particular environment, this explains why one person seems to flourish in a certain setting, while another suffers. Professors Tom Cummings and Cary Cooper have designed a way of understanding the stress process, as explained below:

● Individuals for the most part try to keep their thoughts, emotions and relationships with the world in a 'steady state'.

● Each factor of a person's emotional and physical state has a 'range of stability', in which that person feels comfortable. On the other hand, when forces disrupt one of these factors beyond the range of stability, the individual must act or cope to restore a feeling of comfort.

● An individual's behaviour aimed at maintaining a steady state makes up his or her 'adjustment process', or coping strategies.

A stress is any force that puts a physiological or physical system beyond its range of stability, producing a strain within the individual. Knowledge that a stress is likely to occur constitutes a threat to the individual. A threat can cause a strain because of its meaning to the person.

The above description can be summarized in the small diagram below:

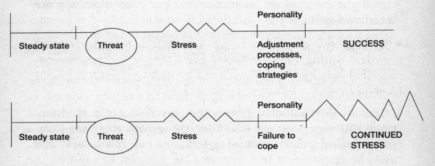

Figure 1: Symptoms of Stress

The Stress Bill

To the individual whose health or happiness has been ravaged by the effects of stress, the costs or 'stress bill' involved are only too clear. Whether manifested as minor complaints or serious ailments such as heart disease, or as social problems such as alcoholism and drug abuse, stress-related problems exact a heavy payment. It has also long been recognized that a family suffers indirectly from the stress problems of one of its members – suffering that takes the form of unhappy marriages, divorces, and spouse and child abuse. But what price do organizations and nations pay for a poor fit between people and their environments? Only recently has stress been seen as contributing to the health costs of companies and countries; but as studies of stress-related illnesses and deaths show, stress is taking a devastatingly high toll on our combined productivity and health.

● Coronary heart disease is the leading cause of death in Britain and 'kills more than 150,000 people each year – one person every three to four minutes. One man in eleven dies of a heart attack before he is sixty-five years old' (Health Education Authority report).

● Days lost from work due to stress-related causes (e.g., heart disease, mental disorders, etc.) during the 1980s represented 34 per cent of all days lost for men and 33 per cent for women.

● In Britain, 5 per cent of men and 12 per cent of women are on tranquillizers.

● In England, general practice consultation rates for mental disorders during 1984 were 300 per 1,000 of the population, exceeded only by coughs, colds and bronchitis. (Source: (1986) *General Household Survey*. London: HMSO.)

● The Confederation of British Industry reported that absenteeism had risen 'alarmingly in recent years in spite of improvements in social and working conditions, income levels and family health'.

● Alcohol abuse is becoming an increasingly severe problem for women. In the 1980s, 1 person in 2.4 who requested help to deal with alcoholism at local British Alcohol Advisory councils was a woman, as compared to 1 in 4 applicants in the 1970s.

In the future, we may also see an increasing trend for employees to consider suing their employers for stress at work. The California Supreme Court upheld its first stress-disability case in the early 1970s and claims now stand at around 3,000 a year. The California Labor Code now states specifically that workers' compensation is allowable for disability or illness caused by 'repetitive mentally or physically traumatic activities extending over a period of time, the combined effect of which causes any disability or need for medical treatment'. California may be the first, but what happens there has a habit of reaching other places.

What are the Symptoms of Stress?

Even though stress can cost a great deal in personal, job and health terms, many of us seem to cope well with the pressures of work and family life encountered daily. But when does stimulating pressure turn into harmful stress? Consider what scientists believe happens to the human body when it is subjected to a strain or pressure of some kind.

As Andrew Melhuish, a physician specializing in stress, has suggested, man is the product of many thousands of years of evolution and in order to survive he was required to respond quickly and physically to dangers. His body 'developed the ability to rev-up' for a short time. As mentioned earlier, Walter Cannon described this mobilization of force as the 'fight or flight' reaction. Primitive man expended this burst of energy and strength in physical activity, such as a life-or-death struggle or a quick dash to safety.

Modern man has retained his hormonal and chemical defence mechanisms through the centuries. But for the most part, people's lifestyle today does not allow physical reaction to the stressors they face. Attacking the boss, hitting an insolent salesman in a store, or taking a club to a broken-down railway engine are not solutions allowed by today's society. (Although such physical responses would create even more problems for most people in real life, it is interesting to note the vicarious appeal of violent physical acts in television and movies for a large part of our modern population.) Today, even the non-aggressive 'flight' reaction would hardly be judged appropriate in most situations. The manager who flees from a tense meeting, and the assembly worker who dashes out in the middle of a shift are likely to suffer the consequences of their actions. Our long-evolved defence mechanisms prepare us for dramatic and rapid action, but find little outlet. The body's strong chemical and hormonal responses are then like frustrated politicians: 'All dressed up with nowhere to go.' David Emanuel highlighted his stress during a new show:

'Yes, God, it's exciting, then you're waiting for what the press have got to say, then waiting for the pictures to see what people have done. And then you come to think, so what! But then, the weak spot comes out, usually it's my throat. The day after a show I usually have a huge ulcer in my throat or I have like a major sore throat.'

Or as Elizabeth Emanuel says:

'You break out in spots in your hair, or whatever. It's your body, because you're pushing it, aren't you, you're pushing like twelve hours a day sometimes, day after day after day, but you know you haven't time to be tired. You've got to say, that's mind over body, to convince yourself you're not tired. But at least you've done it, you've done your best, and it shows. And then you need a weekend, a couple of days, to forget about everything, and then you start the process again.'

The body's 'rev-up' activity is designed to improve perform-ance, but if the stress which launches this activity continues unabated, the body begins to weaken under a bombardment of stimulation and stress-related chemicals. As Derek Jameson reflects from his stress experiences:

'I don't suffer any mental confusion as a result of this pressure – it gets me in the back of the neck. I then go to an osteopath who also does acupuncture, and he's been sticking these needles in me. The steel bands at the back of my neck have been worse over these last few days than at any time I can remember, brought on by stress. But that's where the pressure gets me, in this muscular pain.'

As stress begins to take its toll on the body and mind, a variety of symptoms can result. Doctors have identified a number of symptoms of stress. This usually starts in the first stage with behavioural manifestations, such as some of the following shown in Table 1.

Judy Finnigan of *This Morning* programme experiences some of these symptoms when she is overloaded: 'Problems always seem so enormous when you are lying in bed and you can't get

Table 1: Mental Symptoms of Stress

Constant irritability with people
Feeling unable to cope
Lack of interest in life
Constant, or recurrent fear of disease
A feeling of being a failure
A feeling of being bad or self-hatred
Difficulty in making decisions
A feeling of ugliness
Loss of interest in other people
Awareness of suppressed anger
A feeling of being the target of other people's animosity
Loss of sense of humour
Feeling of neglect
Dread of the future
A feeling of having failed as a person or parent
A feeling of having no one to confide in
Difficulty in concentrating
The inability to finish one task before rushing on to the next
An intense fear of open or enclosed spaces, or of being alone

at them. When there's real work overload, I get very very hyped up, and feel very tense physically, as well as all the many other manifestations of being highly stressed, like I have difficulty in sleeping, body tension and the like.' Elizabeth Emanuel has found that stress affects her after the pressure is removed, such as after a big international show: 'I find physically that as soon as the stress is removed, physical things happen like my hair starts to shed or I come out in spots, or I suddenly get the flu. They always happen after a period of stress and a lot of activity, once I slow down, I just go to pieces.'

If the sources of the stress are not dealt with, the minor behavioural symptoms can turn into minor physical symptoms, such as those in Table 2.

The whole process of stress can be seen in Rick Wakeman's (the rock musician) account of his stressful years:

'I was living in Switzerland, I got divorced and came back. I lost everything that I had basically over there. I was already

Table 2: Physical Symptoms of Stress

Lack of appetite
Craving for food when under pressure
Frequent indigestion or heartburn
Constipation or diarrhoea
Insomnia
Constant tiredness
Tendency to sweat for no good reason
Nervous twitches
Nail-biting
Headaches
Cramps and muscle spasms
Nausea
Breathlessness without exertion
Fainting spells
Frequent crying or desire to cry
Impotency or frigidity
Inability to sit still without fidgeting
High blood pressure

drinking heavily. I was in a band at the time called Yes, which were a very successful band especially in America, and we were very much a "musical band". In the late seventies and early eighties, the punk era was just starting to come in, which personally I thought was great fun. It hit hard what I call "musical bands" like mine, and it became very "out of flavour" for people to buy your records. So suddenly from selling millions of records per year overnight you were down to thousands in four or five days, which would in no way recoup any of the money that the albums and other things had cost, and no way would keep your lifestyle going. Coupled with the divorce and coming back to England, from being a wealthy boy, overnight I came back to nothing. And then suddenly, you realize that you've got this lifestyle that you can't handle. You've probably got a "drink problem" that is manifesting itself even more, because you tend to drink more. You can't cope anymore, really, because you've got nothing to cope with, and you own up and say "Well, you've got to start again and really fight through it." So you've got to live a little bit of a lie, because if you lose your credibility in the entertainment game, you're finished, because nobody likes a loser in the entertainment world. You've got to be seen to be winning all the time.'

If the source or basis of the stress continues even further, then the pressure could trigger a range of stress-related illnesses, such as those identified in Table 3.

Table 3: Ailments Recognized to Have Stress Background

Hypertension: high blood pressure
Coronary thrombosis: heart attack
Migraine
Hay fever and allergies
Asthma
Pruritus: intense itching
Peptic ulcers
Constipation
Colitis
Rheumatoid arthritis
Menstrual difficulties
Nervous dyspepsia:
    flatulence and
    indigestion
Hyperthyroidism: overactive thyroid gland
Diabetes mellitus
Skin disorders
Tuberculosis
Depression
Anxiety

If the pressure of life exceeds your ability to cope, then your bodily predisposition or genetic make-up or early childhood experience will determine which of these stress diseases you will acquire. This whole process of the link between stress and ill health can be seen in Dr Malcolm Carruthers' account of how stress can be implicated in heart disease (see Figure 2).

Obviously, a great deal of the individual's reactions to the stresses of life depends on his or her coping strategies – that is, how he/she deals with the stress – which are a function of our personality and the set of learned copying methods we carry around with us. We can see this process clearly in Figure 1. A

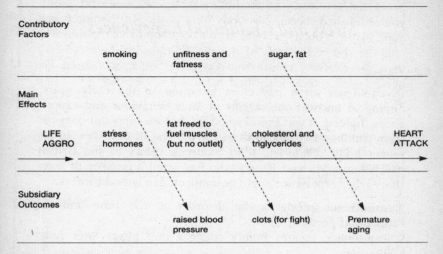

Contributory Factors

smoking   unfitness and fatness   sugar, fat

Main Effects

LIFE AGGRO   stress hormones   fat freed to fuel muscles (but no outlet)   cholesterol and triglycerides   HEART ATTACK

Subsidiary Outcomes

raised blood pressure   clots (for fight)   Premature aging

LIFE AGGRO refers to life 'aggravation': stress agents at work, in the home, etc.

Figure 2: Flight Path to a Heart Attack
(*source*: an adaptation from Malcolm Carruthers, Maudsley Hospital)

stress event or 'crunch point' is any force that puts a psychological or physical factor beyond its range of stability, producing a strain within the individual. Knowledge that a stress is likely to occur constitutes a threat to the individual. A threat can cause a strain or stress reaction because of what it signifies to the person. Whether we are successful or fail to cope with this pressure or crisis is a finely balanced process, which depends to a large extent on how we assess a stressful situation and what coping strategies we select to deal with it. Understanding the way in which we cope with the stresses of life is the principal objective of this book. There is no point in blaming any circumstance or other person for a failure or an unsatisfying mode of living. People must 'own up', take responsibility and choose a more satisfying way to live. Otherwise you will end up like the Queen's subjects in Lewis Carroll's *Through the Looking Glass*: '"A slow sort of country!" said the Queen. "Now here, you see, it takes all the running you can do, to keep in one place. If you want to get somewhere else, you must run at least twice as fast as that!"'

2

Stress and Childhood Experiences

Psychologists often pay close attention to the early years, hoping to uncover the origins of later behaviour and experiences. Indeed, it was Freud who said that we carry our baggage from childhood around with us for the rest of our lives. In his recent book, *Children*, John Santrock refers to the British psychologist Michael Rutter who has listed a number of ways that earlier experience might be connected to later disorders:

1. experience produces the disorder at the time and the disorder persists;
2. experience creates bodily changes that affect later functioning;
3. experience alters patterns of behaviour at the time, which later take the form of a disorder;
4. early experiences can change family relationships and circumstances, which over time lead to a disorder;
5. sensitivities to stress or coping strategies are changed, which then later predispose the person to disorder, or buffer the person from stress;
6. experiences change the child's self-concept or attitudes, which in turn influence behaviour in later circumstances; and
7. experience influences behaviour by affecting the selection of environments or the opening up or closing of opportunities.

Developmental psychologists tend to view young children as often being highly malleable and growing up in a complex social world which they commonly adapt to. Thus, experiences with mothers, fathers, surrogates, siblings and peers, the quality of child-care and schooling and cultural and socio-economic factors, can all affect development. Attachment and early experiences are important contributors to problems and disturbances both in childhood and later on in adulthood. However, although it has become something of a cliché to attribute problems in adulthood to adverse stressful experiences in childhood, we believe that there were some definite links between past and present in the people we interviewed.

Social Origins

Most of the individuals we spoke to came from comfortable middle- or upper-class backgrounds, and rarely linked their social origins with stressful events during childhood. Even so, at least one had experienced degrees of poverty in his early life which had undoubtedly had long-term consequences. Broadcaster and journalist Derek Jameson grew up in a home for waifs and strays, and graphically described his poverty-stricken childhood:

'The home was run by a wonderful old girl called Mrs Wren, Ma Wren – she was the original old lady who lived in a shoe and she raised over seventy kids, abandoned, rejects, illegitimate, orphaned – some even left on her doorstep! She did it without a penny from anyone – there was no Welfare State in the thirties, this was high depression. We all grew up together there in total poverty, even begging for money on the streets. So, I suppose that was a rather stressful situation for a young child to grow up in. You can imagine the mayhem that went on in that household – with all those deprived people.

'I finished up in a hostel for bad boys. I was rubber-stamped "beyond care and control". Remember, I came from a very rough, tough background and the old "beg, borrow and steal" was literally true in no particular order of merit. So I was very much a king of kids, a juvenile delinquent, organizing raids on shops, thieving, fiddling anything to turn a buck. We were selling horse manure. By the time I was seven or eight, I was earning a living, making money. If things got desperate we would go outside the local railway station, Clapton in Hackney, and as the city clerks, the commuters poured off the trains, we used to say "Give us a ha'penny, Mister". Maybe one in twenty would give you a halfpenny and when you got four pence you could buy a loaf of bread. That's one of my earliest memories, begging for money in the streets, so it was a very rough time.'

For Derek Jameson, these traumatic childhood events not

only made him a 'stress addict', but became the prime motivating forces in his striving for wealth and fame:

'I think you can get hooked on the adrenalin. I've lived with stress since the minute I was born. My whole life has been a struggle for survival. I was born poor and hungry so I decided to become rich and famous – not pursuing the demon "ambition", not for material gain, possessions, houses, yachts – just simply to survive. The opposite of poor is rich, isn't it? The opposite of hungry is success. If you've got those two things going for you, you're not going to go hungry and that's really been the motivating force in my life. I've put a million miles between myself and the gutter in the East End where I come from.'

The poet and writer Roger McGough came from a working-class family in Liverpool, and while not subjected to the same degree of poverty, he does remember instances of social class consciousness from his mother:

'I think my parents were ambitious for me, my mother certainly was, not having had an education herself but being intelligent. One of my first memories was when I first went to school. I remember having to write what my dad did for a living. I said he was a docker. I told my mum and she said, "No, he's a stevedore", because that sounds better. So there was always that working-class thing, like cleaning the steps, we always had clean steps, that sort of thing. But, it was all right, I mean she wasn't heavy, I look back and it was happy.'

Like Derek Jameson, Roger McGough has retained his original accent, in his case, Liverpudlian. Indeed, it proved an asset at the beginning of his career, during the 'Swinging Sixties', when working-class heroes become the vogue in the media, and he made his name as one of the Liverpudlian poets and member of the Scaffold pop group. Derek Jameson's East End accent has now become his trademark and has certainly contributed to his success. However, this hasn't always been the case.

'It seemed to me that in order to succeed, I needed to get into an area where there was an egalitarian meritocracy, where it didn't matter where you came from, who your father was, how you spoke, or what your background was. As long as you had talent, drive, interest and enthusiasm, then you would succeed.

I knew that that meant newspapers and media, and that was why I went into journalism. However, throughout most of my career I found being an East End boy with a Cockney accent was still a handicap. Many times throughout my forty years in newspapers, I was bypassed not on the basis of my ability and talent, but simply because someone came along with the right impeccable background, the right old school tie, and the right father. My accent and my class frequently worked against me. I had to overcome these obstacles. For instance, when I was in the race to become editor of the *Daily Mirror*. A friend suggested that I should get the job because I'd achieved great circulation successes against the *Sun* in the north of England (where I was Northern Editor in Manchester). The editorial director responded instantly, "What, with that accent!" Yet the *Mirror* was a Labour newspaper and I was very happy there because I felt safer, more cosy in an environment that was ostensibly working class.

'My accent today, the way I speak, is my fortune – it makes me almost unique. People say that I acquired this accent realizing I could exploit it. But I always say "Brother, if I was going to put on an accent, it wouldn't have been this one!"'

At the other end of the spectrum, coming from a very privileged, wealthy background also evoked some stressful childhood memories for at least one successful personality. Jonathan Dimbleby recounted the dread of his parents' opulence when they visited him at boarding school: 'When I was a teenager, and my father [Richard Dimbleby] came to Charterhouse, my parents were not allowed to turn up in the very nice Rolls-Royce that we had, they had to come in an old battered car which was a Consul, or a Land Rover or some such thing, because I didn't want to be seen as the beneficiary of all that.'

Separation and Loss

Researchers such as Sroufe, Ainsworth and Bowlby have argued that attachment plays a vital role in promoting optimal psychologically healthy development, both in infancy and later in childhood and adulthood. Whether a child receives loving care from his or her mother, father or any other sensitive adult is immaterial; what is important is that the care is consistent and continuous. Although children can withstand brief separations from the individual, they become attached to parents and long-term separations are often difficult for them to cope with. In fact, sometimes this kind of parental separation can be an emotional rather than a physical one.

Although no one we interviewed had experienced the early death of a parent, a number did recount periods in their childhood as being in some way a time of loss or indeed deprivation. Some of them felt disorientated and rootless. The television broadcaster Stuart Hall remembers feeling neglected by his parents who concentrated on their business ventures:

'I was the eldest child of the family. It was always a great secret that was kept from me that the family were Catholic Irish. In those days, it was never owned up to, being Irish . . . Miles Hennessey shipped to dark satanic mills of Lancashire. My father was a baker and married my mother when she was sixteen. My early days were spent in a baker's shop, then eventually another shop and another shop until a factory. I had a brother who was five years younger than me and I tended to act as a surrogate parent for him.

'I became very bored because my parents worked so hard, and I became a rebel. I became a juvenile delinquent, I played truant from school and I was always in trouble. I wanted a mother, mothering, but my mother had no time to spend with me.' As a direct consequence of this, he is now very family orientated and family holidays still include his son and daughter despite both being in their twenties.

It is only in the last decade that researchers have shown any real interest in father–infant relationships. Not surprisingly, what these studies show is that young children not only interact with their fathers, they also form a strong attachment to them. Several of our stress survivors found themselves traumatized by the separation from their fathers, often by war or other circumstances. Roger McGough was a child during the war years in Liverpool:

'I remember things like the war, barrage balloons and air-raid shelters, that sort of side of it. I probably didn't pick up the anxieties of my parents as, at that young age, it seemed quite an exciting time – going into air-raid shelters in the middle of the night.

'I was evacuated for a while with my mother and sister. We all went to North Wales and left my father, who was still working in Liverpool. I do remember at that time developing nervous tics. I saw a girl when I was out one day who had a tic, shrugging a shoulder, I think it was. When I returned home I was "doing it" too. My mother said, "What are you doing that for?" I said, "I saw a girl doing it." She said, "Stop it," but I couldn't! So everyone said that I was a nervous child. You can imagine that perhaps in another background, maybe a nervous, sensitive child would be something to be admired, but it wasn't the case in Liverpool in the fifties – the reaction was "say a prayer".'

Ironically, it was this sensitivity, which was being dampened early in his life, which was essential for his development as a writer: 'It was only later that you get certain sensitivities about things, about language and possibly about situations that you count as a blessing as a writer, but during your youth you didn't because you didn't know what it was. You were always told that you "felt too much" – that you shouldn't.'

Gloria Hunniford, the radio and television personality, viewed frequent separations from her father due to his work commitments as extremely stressful when she was very young:

'Casting my mind back very quickly, ours was a very close-knit Irish family, and one of the early stressful situations that I can remember was my father going away for two weeks, which I thought at the time was the end of the world. I must have been three or four at the time. He had a lot of outside interests, he was a pigeon-fancier and also an amateur magician, so occasionally these interests would take him away from home. I remember when he went away saying to him, "When are you coming home, daddy, will it be late tonight, and I'll not see you until tomorrow?" When he said, "I won't be back for two weeks," as a child that was like an eternity to me. I was very close to both my parents, but I remember thinking that this was dreadful, that he just wouldn't be coming back. I don't remember pining for him every day, it was just like "getting a kick in the stomach", my world seemed to fall apart.'

Long-term effects stemming from the separation from both parents during childhood years were described by Victor Kiam and Derek Jameson. For the American entrepreneur Victor Kiam, the divorce of his parents at the age of four was one of the most crucial events in his life. The age of a child at the time of his/her parents' divorce does appear to be a factor in predicting the subsequent effects of the divorce on the child. According to recent research findings, younger children seem to be affected more negatively, particularly if divorce disrupts the 'attachment bond' between either or both parents. Furthermore, younger children are less able to evaluate their own role in the divorce, the cause, the possible outcomes and so on.

Victor Kiam described the impact his parents' divorce had on him, both in the short and long term:

'I was born in Louisiana, New Orleans; it was a very religious state. There were very few divorces at that time; now, I guess, there's an awful lot more. I was sort of the anomaly among my young peers because of having divorced parents. My grandparents brought me up and they couldn't have been more devoted, but by the age of seven or eight I had developed a sense of being different, a sort of insecurity. When kids would sleep over and there were my grandparents, they'd say, "Where's your mommie and daddy?" and I'd say "They're away." Six months later they might sleep over again and they'd say, "Where's your mommie and daddy?" and they'd still be away. It was a situation in which I perceived myself as being different.

'I remember that there was a family who lived across the street about a block down, when my parents and I were living together. In this family, there were three kids and a mommie and a daddy, and I always thought they were ideally happy. The thought of that family gave me a direction and I said to myself, "I haven't got what they've got but gosh, I *will* be as happy as those other people."

'As life evolved, the lives of those particular parents and the kids became an absolute shambles, and I just said, "How could this have happened?" I related my existence to theirs, and my background, and I just looked on those kids as being so fortunate because, compared to mine, they had such a wonderful environment. It turned out it was quicksand, it didn't exist.

'My mother never recovered from her divorce and never remarried; and my father went through a series of marriages, but never ultimately found happiness. He married five times and had innumerable adventures, not affairs. Whenever he went with one lady, that was it; he was neither a wanderer nor a philanderer.'

As the years passed, Victor Kiam grew closer to his parents and sympathized with their respective predicaments. Nevertheless, their lifestyles and the consequences for his own upbringing once again made him determined not to repeat their pattern:

'As my father got older and I saw his lifestyle, I really had sympathy for his predicament, because it was a predicament. I also learned that I had sympathy for my mother's predicament, a woman who never lost her affection for this man who couldn't relate to her or others. My mother's still alive, I generally call her every day and I think I've been a stalwart mainstay to her passing through this life of ours, because I've been the rock on which she could rely.

'I think looking at my own situation, and also the lifestyles and lives of my parents, that I was absolutely devoted to the idea that I would develop a stable, happy home life. I've been married once, I have three kids and a grandchild, and I think the family is very, very close.'

Studies of institutionalized children illustrate that an experience of many caretakers and differences in the quality of care received from each of them result in children often failing to form attachments. Moreover, their lack of experience of forming reliable and predictable long-term relationships in childhood often leads to difficulties later on in their adult relationships.

Not surprisingly, institutionalization, childhood poverty and deprivation linked to a total rejection by both parents contributed towards thrice-married Derek Jameson's difficulties in forming stable relationships in adulthood, as well as an insatiable hunger to be loved:

'I was born illegitimate and I never knew my father. I grew up in a Home and didn't know who my mother was until I was seven or eight. It was only after the first few years that I discovered that one of the older girls in the Home was in fact my mother. Obviously, it caused me a great deal of confusion because some of my contemporaries didn't have any parents around, others had a mother who might visit once a month. To me, my mother was Elsie and she continued to be Elsie until I was well into my thirties. I never called her mum or mother, and never considered her as a mother. As I said, I was seven or eight before I discovered who she was and at the age of nine the war broke out and I was evacuated. I didn't come back until I was fourteen, and then I was so desperate and determined to become a journalist, I got a job as a messenger boy in Fleet Street.'

Nevertheless, he did form extremely close life-long bonds with at least two of the other children who shared his childhood struggle for survival in the Homes and begging on the streets of London:

'I think you form a bond with kids like that, probably even stronger than blood ties. The two closest persons to me were Lenny Frost and a girl called Peggy Crotty, who changed her name to Pat. Lenny works in a night bakery at the moment. He did over twenty years in a furniture factory. He grew up alongside me, a bit older than myself.

'Pat was the closest person to me. She married a marvellous character in the East End called Stan Kemp, a former marine. They set up home in the East End, raised three kids and were working as night cleaners in a bank until three or four years ago when she died of cancer. I knew she was dying, but I didn't know how serious it was or how long it would be before she died, as I was up in Manchester for much of the time. I didn't see very much of her, maybe once every two or three years, but I knew she was dying and went to see her.

'A few weeks later on a Monday afternoon, I wasn't working, I was editor of the *News of the World* and was off duty on the Monday. In the early afternoon, I got terrible pains, the most agonizing pains, my whole body felt as if it was being torn apart, quite indescribable agony. I was lying on my bed for a couple of hours writhing in agony, when the pain lifted just as quickly as it came – just disappeared. About an hour later, the phone rang and I said to Ellen, my lady, "That'll be Pat's died." It was one of her sons to say his mother had died that afternoon, so I'd obviously picked up her death pains – but we weren't related, there were no blood ties. I put it down to a very close attachment. I think those relationships you form under conditions of extreme adversity, as a child struggling for survival, are every bit as durable and powerful as any normal blood relationship.'

Furthermore, he acknowledges that his choice of career and driving ambition ultimately stems from his desire to be recognized and loved – a need sadly never fulfilled during his childhood:

'Look at my working day, up at five-thirty to do two hours of live broadcasting, where I'm talking to ten million people from that studio every morning – fifty million a week. Then I may well go and make a television programme that's watched by another ten million, so I'm conscious that sixty million people a week are tuning into me.

'If you can do that without the slightest tremor or nerves or hesitation, then that is an achievement. And, of course, because I felt rejected and abandoned and lost as a child, I was desperate for the love, affection and goodwill of the people around me. I think that my life as an editor, broadcaster and communicator was dictated by my need to make people know that I exist and care for me. It's really a search for love. That's why I get so deeply hurt when anyone rubbishes me.'

Parental Influences

As we have already illustrated, parental influences (or lack of them) can prove particularly crucial during the formative years. Furthermore, we discovered that *how* the parents of some of our stress survivors coped with pressure had often influenced the coping style adopted by their offspring. For example, Helen Fraser, the publishing executive, very much identified with the way her mother had to cope with a husband with a drinking problem and a nervous disposition.

'I remember that when my father had drunk too much he wasn't violent at all. He would be unsteady on his feet, sleepy, maudlin, very affectionate to young women in the vicinity – I mean, he was quite charming. But I think the main thing I remember was the fact that he'd had a very severe nervous breakdown when I was about two. I don't personally remember anything about it at all, but I know it was a frightful family trauma. What I do remember was always the feeling that my mother was in charge and that I was kind of second in charge. So, for instance, if we ever went on holiday, my father hated travelling, and we did travel a certain amount in my adolescence. Anyway, he would panic. We'd be driving in the car and he'd be sitting in the front saying, "We'll never get there, it'll be dark, we won't find our way – oh God, oh God." He'd be absolutely panicking, and my mother and I would be saying, "It's all right, don't worry, we'll be fine." So I think it's probably influenced the way I react in a crisis. I know one of the things that people who work for me say is that they like the fact that I don't panic. Obviously, in publishing, terrible things can go wrong – you've just published a book when you discover that the warehouse has failed to distribute or whatever. Though I mind about those sorts of things, and am determined to put them right, I don't "awfulize" and "catastrophize", I tend to say, "OK, that's really bad, but never mind, let's see what we can do about it." People have told me that I therefore tend to produce a calmer and more productive environment, because I'm not shrieking and having hysterics.'

As Nancy Friday said in her book *My Mother, My Self*: 'When I stopped seeing my mother with the eyes of a child, I saw the woman who helped me give birth to myself.' Similarly, Helen Fraser's mother continued to act as an important role model:

'My father was very much a non-coping adult, which meant that my mother was a gritty realist. She was the one who went to see the tax man, the one who dealt with the bank manager, the one who actually read the bank statements, the one who would go and earn money to fish us out of the soup. So, I suppose, I have an image of women as being very, very competent, very risk orientated, being people who in the end keep everything going. While my father, while obviously very creative, very clever, very funny, and very charming, was not a fully adult human being.'

A number of those we interviewed emphasized the importance of 'parental nurturing' in heightening their confidence and security, which had long-lasting effects.

'I was the apple of my mother's eye,' said politician and broadcaster Austin Mitchell. 'She always did things for us which no man should be taught to expect from a wife today. It heightened our security. I was brought up in an environment where you could find your feet and develop without being challenged. Therefore, when I found that I was good at university, I was good at teaching or eventually when I found I was good at communication in the media – I could do them all and never felt competitive about it or insecure.'

However, although Jonathan Dimbleby recounted that both his parents were immensely talented and sensitive in the way in which they brought him up, he remembers finding it extremely difficult, and occasionally stressful, having to cope with being the son of such·a famous father:

'I always felt acutely aware of being Richard Dimbleby's son, very aware that I would be judged as his son, that I had a particular responsibility which I frequently failed to fulfil and to behave in ways that he would not be upset or embarrassed by.

'When I was a child, we had a chauffeur and if we'd been to a pantomime or the theatre, we'd go into a restaurant afterwards. I would prefer to just go and have a little bit to eat and then go and sit quietly in the back seat of the car, while they went on eating in the restaurant. I remember being fearfully embarrassed by the prominence of my father, the attention he attracted. I recall going as a family to the Arthur Askey Show and the management announcing that in the audience they had a famous and great man, Richard Dimbleby. The spotlight would then come on to him where we were sitting, and I would sit right down, cringing under the chair out of acute self-consciousness. I didn't enjoy that side of his life.'

These childhood experiences are still very vivid and he closely empathizes with children whose famous parents make them highly vulnerable in terms of media attention:

'When I read now about the offspring of famous people who are now focused upon in a disgraceful way in the gutter press, I have an immense sympathy for these young people and for their parents. I mean, the tragedies like Channon's daughter and the grotesque treatment of that, I find shameful and disgusting, because I as a child was in the early stages of that process. It wasn't anything like as intense a glare, but the glare on my father was absolutely extraordinary because he was "Mr Television".'

Education

Although education in one form or another was crucial to most of those we interviewed, very few actually recalled significant stressful experiences while at school. Occasionally, individuals recalled the isolation they felt on moving to a new school. According to Joanna Foster, Chair of the Equal Opportunities Commission:

'When I was about thirteen, I was sent to a girls' boarding school and I went in the middle of the year. Therefore, I joined a group that had got themselves established – they were a very bright group and I was bottom of the pile. That's something that's lived with me ever since, I've always seemed to be at the bottom of a bright group rather than at the top of the less bright group. And, it's a great debate in my mind. I see it with my own daughter, and wonder which is it better to be? It does difficult things for your self-confidence because you feel, "They're all much brighter than I am." On the other hand, you need to ponder whether one is able to actually stand back and say, "It's a miracle that I'm here at all!" That way, it encourages you to grow. I'm still wrestling with that one really.'

Helen Fraser, on the other hand, remembered the most traumatic year of her adolescence as being her fourteenth when she went to an American school while her father had a visiting professorship:

'It was a very difficult year for me, because I was a retiring, quiet, studious fourteen-year-old, not very sociable and suddenly I was thrust into this strange environment. This was the early 1960s, so it was America at its most conventional, very "dating orientated", and I was in a class of people two years older than me because that was the level of my work.

'I felt very socially inadequate there. I can remember my mother saying to me, "Now Helen, don't you think it's time you wore a tight skirt and got some high heels?" – you know, isn't it sort of time you grew up? It was so wonderful when the 1960s proper started, as it suited me just splendidly. Suddenly you didn't spend hours putting your hair in curlers, you could listen to the music you wanted to, wear the clothes you wanted. There was none of that business any more about how you have to conform, and be the right sort of tootsie girl for everybody else.'

Unfortunately for Jonathan Dimbleby, his boarding-school environment failed to protect him from the stigma of being 'Mr Television's' son:

'As a child at school, being the son of a famous father is not an advantage. You get the reprieves, the refrains – the phrase I'm searching for is "Just because you are Richard Dimbleby's son, doesn't mean you can . . .", which would come not only from other children but also from some of the teachers as well.'

Products of the Past

Certainly, for some of our stress survivors, traumatic experiences in childhood had indeed shaped their behaviours and attitudes in adulthood. What was interesting was that all of them were obviously very aware of these effects and had rationalized and, in many cases, actively changed their behaviour accordingly.

Lack of parental roles and attachment for individuals such as Derek Jameson had led to difficulties in sustaining marital relationships in later life. For others, parental neglect and divorce of parents had made them determined not to repeat the pattern in their own lives and ensured heavy commitment to marital and family relationships. Not surprisingly, individuals also tended to identify with the 'stronger' parent who often acted as an important and lasting adult role model, even after their death. As Nancy Friday wrote in *My Mother, My Self*: 'The debt of gratitude we owe our mother and father goes forward, not backward. What we owe our parents is the bill presented to us by our children.'

3

Stress and Personality

Given the pressures of life and the experiences of many people, particularly those in the public eye, it is surprising that some people are infinitely better able to cope with the enormous demands on them, while others are not as effective. Why does a minor event tip one person over the edge, yet is barely noticed by another? Ralph Waldo Emerson in 1870 may have got at the essence of this in one of his poems: 'we boil at different degrees.' Effectively, our personality, and perhaps our philosophy of life, act as moderators between the stresses and the strains. They help us to mediate the pressures and select the most appropriate coping strategies. But what is personality, and what kind of personality and philosophy of life are likely to be most prevalent among stress survivors?

'Personality' is a word frequently used in everyday conversation. We may say 'X is lacking in personality', meaning he strikes us as rather insipid, or 'Y has a very dynamic personality', conveying an image of energy and activity. Everyone knows what is meant by it, and there is usually no problem about using the word in this context. Strangely, however, it is very difficult to define precisely what is meant by the term 'personality', and hence to define exactly what it is that we are talking about. It obviously has something to do with the impact or impression a person makes; the way he or she relates to others and the environment. This meaning is reflected in the derivation of the word from the Latin *persona*, the mask worn by Roman actors to convey the role they were playing. As used by modern psychologists, the term has a somewhat wider connotation. Perhaps the best way to think of it is as the total effect of all the skills, abilities, attributes and experiences of the individual. This means that characteristics such as motivation, values and skills are all part of personality. As Ernest Hilgard and his colleagues in their book *Introduction to Psychology* suggest:

Personality, as studied by the psychologist, may be defined as the characteristics and ways of behaving that determine a person's unique adjustments to the environment. The fact that a man eats, sleeps and works does not define his personality; his personality is defined by what he eats, how he sleeps, and what is distinctive about his work patterns. Hence individuality and uniqueness are essential to the definition.

The significance of one's personality in creating or minimizing stress can be seen in many everyday studies. Consider a number of individuals waiting for service at a bank-teller's window. John's impatience is clear: he shuffles his feet, strains to see what is happening ahead of him, sighs in exasperation and aims angry looks at the clerk. In contrast, Susan would appear the epitome of patience and calm as she waits, her face composed, a slight smile upon her lips. But a sharp observer would detect the tightening of her jaw and the tic at the corner of one eye as Susan attempts to conceal her anger. Both John and Susan may be paying an emotional and even physical toll as they wait. Their reactions, though different, are both totally unlike that of Mark, who is truly unconcerned about the wait. He gazes out of the bank window, interested in the flow of life on the street, enjoying the chance to pause for a moment. Just behind him, Louise is using the time to jot down a shopping list and plan what she will cook for dinner.

The personalities and resultant coping styles of the four people described above act together to determine whether the same situation induces a stress response in each. For example, both John and Susan are experiencing varying levels of anxiety as they wait and, furthermore, neither has found a coping style to relieve this reaction. Mark's relaxed personality is naturally such that he has no need to adjust to the situation, while Louise who, like John and Susan, can find waiting stressful, has learned to cope by occupying herself with a useful task, which makes her feel more in control of her time.

This everyday situation should make us aware of the significance of our personality in dealing with the pressures and stresses of life. But what personality types do we find among our stress survivors, what characteristics do they seem to have in common and what philosophy of life do they adhere to?

Type A Personalities

The most definite characteristic that we were able to establish about our stress survivors is that they are predominantly Type As, that is, they engage in a lifestyle that is hard driving, time conscious, ambitious and consumed with achievement and work. The whole concept of Type A behaviour was developed by Meyer Friedman and Ray Rosenman, two American cardiologists, who found that their coronary patients behaved in very similar ways: they were extremely competitive, high achieving, aggressive, hasty, impatient and restless. They were characterized by explosive speech patterns, tenseness of facial muscles and appearing to be under time pressure. These individuals were described as 'Type A' personality types as opposed to the more relaxed 'Type Bs', who had low risks of coronary heart disease and a more passive lifestyle. Type As have been described as people so deeply involved and committed to their work that other aspects of their lives are relatively neglected.

Friedman and Rosenman identified Type A characteristics in their book *Type A Behaviour and Your Heart*, and outlined the following characteristics of Type A personality.

1. Possessing the habit of explosively accentuating various key words in ordinary speech without real need, and tending to utter the last few words of sentences far more rapidly than the opening words. Friedman and Rosenman believe the first habit reflects underlying aggression or hostility, while the second 'mirrors your underlying impatience with spending even the time required for your own speech'.
2. Always moving, walking and eating rapidly.
3. Feeling or revealing to others an 'impatience with the rate at which most events take place'. Finding it 'difficult to restrain from hurrying the speech of others and resorting to the device of saying very quickly, over and over again, "uh huh, uh huh", or saying "yes yes, yes yes", to someone who is talking', urging him to hurry up. Often finishing the sentences of persons speaking.
4. Often attempting to do two or more things at the same time, such as thinking about an irrelevant subject when

listening to someone else speak. 'Similarly, if while golfing or fishing you continue to ponder business or professional problems or while using an electric razor you attempt also to eat your breakfast or drive your car or if while driving your car you attempt to dictate letters for your secretary.' Rosenman and Friedman describe this 'polyphasic' activity as one of the most common traits of the Type A individual.

5. Finding it difficult 'to refrain from talking about or turning any conversation to themes which have personal interest. At times when this manoeuvre fails, pretending to listen but really remaining preoccupied with these personal thoughts.'

6. Almost always feeling vaguely guilty when attempting to relax or do nothing for even just a few hours.

7. No longer noticing the more interesting or lovely things encountered during the day.

8. Not having 'any time to spare to become the things worth being because you are so preoccupied with getting the things worth having'.

9. Attempting to 'schedule more and more in less and less time'. Making fewer allowances for unforeseen events which might disrupt the schedule. Also having a 'chronic sense of time urgency' – a core aspect of the Type A personality.

10. 'On meeting another severely afflicted Type A person, instead of feeling compassion for his affliction you find yourself compelled to "challenge" him. This is a telltale trait because no one arouses the aggressive and/or hostile feelings of one Type A subject more quickly than another Type A subject.'

11. Resorting to 'certain characteristic gestures or nervous tics' such as clenching fists, banging a hand upon a table for emphasis.

12. Becoming increasingly committed to translating and evaluating personal activities and the activities of others in terms of 'numbers'.

Rosenman and Friedman also outlined the following characteristics as indicating the Type B personality:

1. Being 'completely free of all the habits and exhibiting none of the traits of the Type A personality'.

2. Never suffering from time urgency and impatience.
3. Harbouring no 'free-floating hostility' and feeling no need to impress others with your achievements or accomplishments unless the situation demands it.
4. Playing in order to find relaxation and fun, not to demonstrate achievement at any cost.
5. Being able to work without agitation, 'relax without guilt'.

The following questionnaire highlights most of the aspects of Type A behaviour that we found prevalent in most of our stress survivors. You might find it useful in identifying your own Type A behaviour.

Type A Behaviour

Circle one number for each of the fourteen questions below, which best reflects the way you behave in your everyday life. For example, if you are always on time for appointments, on question 1 you would circle a number between 7 and 11. If you are usually more casual about appointments you would circle one of the lower numbers between 1 and 5.

Casual about appointments	1 2 3 4 (5) 6 7 8 9 10 11	Never late
Not competitive	1 2 3 4 5 6 7 8 (9) 10 11	Very competitive
Good listener	1 2 3 4 5 (6) 7 8 9 10 11	Anticipates what others are going to say (nods, attempts to finish for them)
Never feels rushed (even under pressure)	1 2 3 4 5 6 (7) 8 9 10 11	Always rushed
Can wait patiently	1 2 3 4 5 6 7 (8) 9 10 11	Impatient while waiting
Takes things one at a time	1 2 3 4 5 6 7 8 (9) 10 11	Tries to do many things at once, thinks about what will do next
Slow deliberate talker	1 2 3 4 5 6 7 8 9 (10) 11	Emphatic in speech, fast and forceful

Cares about satisfying him/ herself no matter what others may think	1 2 (3) 4 5 6 7 8 9 10 11	Wants good job recognized by others
Slow doing things	1 2 3 4 5 6 (7) 8 9 10 11	Fast (eating, walking)
Easy going	1 2 3 4 5 6 7 8 (9) 10 11	Hard driving (pushing yourself and others)
Expresses feelings	1 (2) 3 4 5 6 7 8 9 10 11	Hides feelings
Many outside interests	1 (2) 3 4 5 6 7 8 9 10 11	Few interests outside work/home
Unambitious	1 2 3 4 5 6 7 8 9 (10) 11	Ambitious
Casual	1 2 3 4 5 6 7 (8) 9 10 11	Eager to get things done

Scoring: The range of possible scores is from 14 to 154, with the average score of 84. The higher the score, the higher your Type A behaviour. People over 90 are in the moderate Type A range, with those above 120 moving into high Type A behaviour. (95)

Source: an adaptation of Bortner's Type A Scale

It is interesting to note that a link between high-status jobs and Type A behaviour has been found in many studies. For example, one study looked at 943 white-collar, middle-class males in Buffalo, New York. The men came from five different work settings – administrative and professional staff of a state health agency; supervisory personnel from a public-service organization; officers from trade unions; faculty staff from a major private university; and administrative officers from a large banking corporation. Not only was the Type A behaviour pattern related to occupational status as measured by rank, level of occupational prestige and income, it was also found to be significantly related to rapid career achievement as indicated by rank and income relative to age. A review of a number of studies bears out the connection between Type A personality and high occupational status. Type As tend to describe their jobs as having more responsibility, longer hours and heavier workloads than do Type Bs. Despite these factors, Type As in general do not report more job dissatisfaction, anxiety or depression than do Type Bs.

Among our stress survivors we found a range of the characteristics described above. Elizabeth Emanuel, the dress designer, suggested:

'I'd rather be under stress and have lots of things going on. On days when there's nothing going on, it's a nightmare. You know, it is a real buzz to be busy, like an adrenalin buzz. Even *now* we get excited about a project or something; the pressure is there, the stress is there, but it actually gives you more energy.'

Broadcaster Pamela Armstrong agrees, feeling that she *needs* the stimulation and pressure:

'There are some people who actually need that kind of excitement in their lives, and I am perhaps one of those. I'm the sort of person who wouldn't respond well to having less stimulation, I would be the type of person who would be stressed by inactivity – I certainly don't seem to be stressed in my life by a high level of activity.'

This sense of enjoyment at work, where work becomes indistinguishable from living, is another feature of our Type A survivors. Jonathan Dimbleby reflects this aspect, which is a consistent feature of the responses we had:

'I don't find it [his lifestyle] stressful, in the sense in which people will say to me that "your job is stressful", because an awful lot of my life is my work. I've got a lot of projects running of one kind or another. Is it more ambition, is it a sense of needing to put my mark on the world? I don't know. The activity itself is so stimulating that you can't do without the stimulus. Is it because you're paid well? I don't know what the reason or answers are. I don't actually ask myself that question very much. Yes, I suppose I need the stimulus, they used to call me the "roadrunner", everyone says it's almost a kind of joke, the workaholic thing. I think those are nonsense notions myself, I'm a workaholic in the sense that I don't make an easy distinction between working and living, because I enjoy what is called my work!'

This theme is reinforced yet again by Sir Terence Conran:

'I have no interest in what people would call leisure-time activities, my work is my hobby. When you're lucky enough to do the sort of things I do, whether it's designing or writing, it's all work in the conventional sense, but I would do them for no reward if that is what was offered. I mix problems at home and work. I am actually one of those rarish people who probably works seven days a week and the reason that I do this is because I have a great diversity of different things that I do, and practically all of them I enjoy – work I look on as an enjoyment.'

Living on the Type A knife-edge is certainly taxing, but its prophylactic effects of enjoyment and satisfaction may actually act as a moderating factor, as Austin Mitchell, MP, suggests:

'I find my best coping strategy is to work harder. I am not a very well-organized person, I spread myself too thinly across the landscape and try to do too many things, but I get satisfaction from them. It's the constant activity that gives me satisfaction and interest, and keeps me awake and alive – I certainly don't feel stress and strain from it.'

Although these Type As enjoy their job, they don't always like the frenetic lifestyle or long hours or the long reports and documents they frequently have to involve themselves in. Victor Kiam, the President of the Remington Corporation, highlighted his frenetic pace while on a trip to London:

'Yesterday, I flew from the States to England. I was asked if I could read the news on the early morning news programme, the following morning. I had to get up at five-forty-five a.m. to be there at six-forty-five, and then I went on about seven-fifteen, but I didn't know what time I was going on. I'd just come over that one day from the States, so if you related that I got up at midnight in the States, I wasn't working on many hours of sleep. Then after the news programme, I had a number of interviews with newspapers, magazines, business meetings in the morning and then I went to luncheon at Wimbledon. My day had only just begun.'

Or as Sir Terence Conran reports:

'I don't enjoy reading long reports and certain documents, but I have to do it. If you are the chairman of a group this size [i.e. Storehouse], you have an endless amount of paperwork that you have to consume, and every weekend I take a carrier bag of paper with me. I start work at eight-fifteen a.m. and I finish at seven p.m. I don't usually take work home in the week, I just take it at weekends and do it Saturday and Sunday. It usually depends on what is happening at the weekends, like the children coming or guests, but I've usually got enough work for probably about one and a half days at the weekend. I do a lot of other things other than business, I do design work and write books. I have always worked a seven-day week, I've always been doing things in my life that I wanted to do, I think that's the difference. An awful lot of people do their work simply to get through life, and earning some money to keep body and soul together. Some people do it as a chore, but if you'd been doing something you want to do, then it isn't a chore.'

But the long hours and frantic pace of life seem to be balanced by an attitude of mind that minimizes what Friedman and Rosenman would term the 'coronary-prone' nature of being Type A. For example, there are many stress survivors who feel that their family helps to mediate this fast pace of living. Eddie Shah, the entrepreneur and founder of *Today* newspaper, finds the family an important source of strength:

'I have learned two things in life. One, don't waste your life, and two, the importance of how much my family actually means to me. I always build time in for my family in my busy schedule. I usually don't get out of bed until about eight-thirty in the morning, so I am a late riser. I come into work about ten. I then try and go home between five-thirty and six, and I try to do this regularly every night. I then leave home at about nine p.m., so I give myself two and a half to three hours with my kids and Jennifer, my wife. Then I come back to work again. Then I'm on the computer or I go to the presses or something, and I work through until three in the morning. This provides me with "thinking time", while the rest of the world sleeps. But family time is essential.'

There are also those who have realized that they have to manage their own lifestyles, because nobody else will do it for them. In fact, many Type A survivors have learned that the hard way, and by their middle age have adapted and, indeed, are trying to educate the next generation. Jonathan Powell, Controller of BBC1 TV, reflects this new awareness:

'There is the kind of corporate culture (in the entertainment industry), where people need to show they'll go to Afghanistan at the drop of a hat. And there are always people who are prepared to do that, because they love it. They need to be educated to the dangers of being like that, and also probably that you can't sustain it over a period of forty years. I suspect that most people of thirty or something, don't realize that. I certainly didn't when I was thirty, it just didn't occur to me that I couldn't carry on like that. Organizations take advantage of that in the way they schedule people, and what they expect of them, so I think it's got to be a two-fold thing. I don't know what advice you'd give to these people [i.e., Type As], because I suspect it would be relatively useless. I think organizations should take much more responsibility for how they "feed off" whatever it is in those people, that leads them to be like that.'

The Hardy Personality

While the Type A personality may help us to understand the lifestyle or behavioural patterns of our stress survivors, it still doesn't fully help us to understand why some Type As have heart attacks and other stress manifestations, and others, like our stress survivors in this book, manage to cope. Suzanne Kobasa, a psychologist from the City University of New York, has developed a theory which attempts to explain this phenomenon.

The theory states that 'among persons facing significant stressors, those high in *Hardiness* will be significantly less likely to fall ill, either mentally or physically, than those who lack hardiness or who display alienation, powerlessness and threat in the face of change'. The key attribute – hardiness – is defined as a personality style that expresses commitment, control and challenge. '*Commitment* is the ability to believe in the truth, importance and interest of who one is and what one is doing and, thereby, the tendency to involve oneself fully in the many situations of life, including work, family, interpersonal relationships and social institutions.' *Control* is defined as the 'tendency to believe and act as if one can influence the course of events. Persons with control seek explanations for why something is happening with emphasis on their own responsibility and not in terms of other actions or fate.' The third aspect of the hardy personality, *challenge*, is based on the individual's 'belief that change, rather than stability, is the normative mode of life'. In terms of the 'challenge' aspect, an individual looks for stimulation, change and opportunities with an openness of mind and willingness to experiment.

Professor Kobasa suggests that hardiness leads to a type of coping:

Keeping specific stressors in perspective, hardy individuals' basic sense of purpose in life allows them to ground events in an understandable and varied life course. Knowing that one has the resources with which to respond to stressors, hardy individuals' underlying sense of control allows them to appreciate a well-exercised coping repertoire. Seeing stressors as potential opportunities for change, challenge enables hardy individuals to see even undesirable events in terms of possibility rather than threat.

In a retrospective study of middle- and upper-level executives, Suzanne Kobasa found support for the idea that executives with high stress but low illness levels show more hardiness than similar executives with high stress and high illness levels. The healthier executives have a 'stronger commitment to self, an attitude of vigourness toward the environment, [and] a sense of meaningfulness' than those executives suffering ill health. The hardiness theory emphasizes once again the importance of the individual response to stress factors in the environment.

Most of our stress survivors were hardy personalities, enjoying the challenge, control and commitment. As Sir Terence Conran indicated:

'I think I thrive on pressure, I think it's probably got something to do with some characteristics of adrenalin, and when the adrenalin is flowing it makes you more active. You can deal with things in a much more positive way, and when the adrenalin stops flowing, then you find problems much more difficult to deal with. I don't think one actively seeks "over-activity", no, but I know that from those moments in my life when you know things are rushing along, I seemed to be able to cope better, than when you go into a sort of lull.'

The challenge element came out again in Eddie Shah's comments:

'I wouldn't say I try and create stress, I hustle things along when I need to. I think in business I have a sense of timing, because I know that there are times when you have just got to walk away from something. But, I find, it's when nothing's happening, it's when business has come to a stop, doing "very well, thank you", that I get very edgy and ratty. The reason I do new things all the time is because I love the challenge of what I do.'

Austin Mitchell reinforces these sentiments: 'In a sense, there is an excitement from the danger of doing too much, it makes me feel alive and gives me more interest in life.'

Unfortunately, a number of our stress survivors feel that there is little challenge in most aspects of ordinary life, which is what they feel creates the stress; people are obliged to work, rather than seeing work as pleasure and challenge. Eddie Shah illustrates this:

'You look at most people, they go to work either by tube or by car, they're just going into work. They've got to be in for eight o'clock or eight-thirty, they go to their desk and they sit there and they work. They read magazines about people like me and they say, "It must be marvellous to have a nice big house and a big garden, he flies his own plane, he drives a brand-new BMW. He can do most things he wants, he's got the money to do it. He can go and meet Prime Ministers, and can do most things – it must be a marvellous life." Right, that's the achievement everybody wants, you know. "He runs his own business, he's got a lot of newspapers, he's expanding and growing and going into television. What a life. I'd love to have a life like that." Well, I have that life and I enjoy it. It's not being a workaholic, it's actually enjoying what I do. And why should you stop doing what you enjoy? The main thing is when it gets to the day when I don't enjoy it, then I'll stop. A definition of a workaholic is not somebody who necessarily enjoys it and does it, it's somebody who does it because they feel obliged to do it.'

Another important characteristic of a hardy personality is that they tend to be individuals who perceive themselves to be in control, what we in the (psychological) trade describe as having an 'internal locus of control'. The concept of locus of control was first developed in the mid-1960s by Professor Rotter, who looked at the extent to which individuals feel they have control over situations. Someone with an *internal* locus of control believes he or she has control over what happens, and that his or her decisions and actions influence personal outcomes. In contrast, someone with an *external* locus of control believes he or she has little influence upon situations and that outcomes are, for the most part, determined by fate or chance. 'Internals' are more confident that they can effect a change in the world around them, while 'externals' believe they have little or no power to produce change.

The locus-of-control theory has received a great deal of attention in recent years. Within the education field, 'internals' are frequently associated with academic success and greater motivation to achieve. Studies of psychological adjustment and coping abilities have shown internals to be less anxious and better able to deal with frustration. The 'external', in contrast, appears 'less psychologically healthy'. In addition, a number of studies have suggested that a person's perceived control over a situation is an advantage in managing environmental stress agents and situations.

Most, if not all, of our stress survivors are 'internals'. Indeed, only when events occur beyond their control do they tend to feel stressed. As Pamela Armstrong indicated: 'When I am in situations where I have no control, no actual real control over it, then it seems unending, and is very very stressful.'

On balance, our stress survivors were 'in control', living in the present and future, and not in the past – even though the past affected them. They were able, in effect, to live in St Augustine's three social time zones: 'There are only three times, a present of things past; a present of things present; and a present of things future.'

Success from Insecurity or Failure

Quite a number of our stress survivors seemed to feel that part of their success in coping in life was due to some basic insecurity or past failure. Derek Jameson, for example, still feels that somebody is judging him:

'Never, ever in my life, have I felt secure, or cosy or relaxed or comfortable. You're looking over your shoulder all the time, thinking that they're gonna get me or find me out, but I'm sure that's always there. Me, I always say, "Me? Do they mean Me?" – it became my catch-phrase.'

Stuart Hall, the radio and TV presenter, expresses the same sentiments, but particularly about having failure experiences:

'I think there are great milestones in one's life, particularly failure. I think when people are lucky enough to have failed, and been given another chance of success, people get to know themselves very well. It's only a big mega, mega failure. People who have had success all their lives, or who have been happy all their lives, or who have been content, or who seem untroubled by the everyday worries, now they're the people I would worry about. It's only by having the troughs and peaks in life that you can actually realize who you are and what life's really about.'

There are also those who think that experiencing stress and anxiety is what makes life worthwhile. Roger McGough, the poet and writer, thinks it stimulates him and provides him with 'food for literary thought':

'There's also that sort of free-floating anxieties that people talk about, like when I'm whistling and happy, not a care in the world, then I sit next to someone on the Tube who's in stress or pain, and they pass it on to me and I go away worrying about everything. So, that's the stress that is always there, a sort of anxiety, a transient sort of thing, a general pressure that we all have. I don't see that as necessarily a bad thing. I'm a nervous sort of person, I speak fast when I'm nervous, that's a sign of anxiety, but I don't necessarily see that as a bad trait. I wouldn't want to change it, because it is a part of what makes me what I am.'

Indeed, Derek Jameson sees what others would want to hide as a real plus in life:

'I've never hidden my origins, but I've met many people in my life who do. You could almost say it's a characteristic of British life that you should appear to be solid, comfortable, respectable middle-class, even to the point of changing the accent. There are many people in the media who speak "properly", which I don't, who I know from the point of view of their background, that their natural voice and accent would be not dissimilar from my own. I've never tried to hide my background, in fact, I've made a virtue of it. I've always been intensely proud of the fact that I come from the "bottom of the heap". I always think that if I can encourage and inspire others who are born in total deprivation to get ahead of the game, then that's probably the best thing I've done in my life. It's been some sort of example to others in the same situation.'

Drive and Energy

In addition to being hardy personalities, who have some element of insecurity or vulnerability, the stress survivors also have masses of drive and energy. Eddie Shah illustrates this in his reflections about his father's view of him:

'My father said, "The thing about you, is that you're one of those few people in the world who has enormous energy, and when you have energy like that, you can do anything. That's the one end of the scale," he said. "People who have that sort of energy can change the shape of the world, and it's more powerful than an atom bomb going off." He said, "I don't know what it is, it's certain people at certain times, and something just goes, and they just have the ability to transmit this energy into thousands or millions of people. When you get into something," he said, "you just take everybody with you." People watching you on TV, they sit there. Now, I'm just saying something that my father said, and I know when I get going, I mean nothing stops me. I just do it.'

A high degree of energy is an important characteristic of our stress survivors. It was singled out by our sample as an essential quality if the challenges and frustrations of the pressures to achieve some personal goal are to be overcome. Indeed, in their book *The Change Makers*, Cary Cooper and Peter Hingley found that this was a common trait in all of society's change agents, as Sir Michael Edwardes highlighted in that book: 'All change agents have one thing in common, provided they are the right people for that role, they all have drive. This is the one thing they must have. They don't need a high intellect, but drive, yes, it's crucial.'

This energy or drive provides our stress survivors with an opportunity to commit themselves, to achieve some personal standards. Work provides them with a foundation on which to achieve some individual goals, which could have some wider social or personal meaning, a philosophy of life. This philosophy or attitude to living helps to protect them, to support them from the rigours of daily pressures and stresses.

Attitude to Living

Even though most of the stress survivors consider themselves to be autonomous operators, individualists, they see their actions as part of a much wider life plan; most important of all, they are 'positivists'. The vast majority of them are 'eternal optimists', who cannot or will not accept failure, or do not want to see 'the negatives' in life. They constantly turn adverse situations into positive ones. As Gloria Hunniford, radio and TV personality, reflected:

'The last couple of years have been very good years in many ways, in that I'm basically a very happy person. I always try to turn the bright side of the stone up, it's very hard to flatten me down. I get down, but I'll rise up again and, in fact, I've been blessed with a very cheerful attitude to things. I am not a morose person. Yes, things get me down, I have a really good bawl, but I get rid of it, then I bounce right back again. I am resilient, and also my kids have always been supportive and caring.'

This is even the case for those stress survivors who have had marriage break-ups, as Linda Kelsey, former editor of *Cosmopolitan* and currently editor of *She*, indicates: 'I've always had this feeling that things will turn out all right. I'm not cynical. Because I had the fortunate example of my parents and their happy marriage. Despite my own marriage breaking down and having several relationships with other people that eventually broke up, I always think, "Oh well, something else will turn up."'

Being positive extends to being prepared to make important and risky decisions, which all stress survivors seem skilled at doing. Victor Kiam neatly sums up this attitude to living which seems prevalent in many of our survivors:

'No decision is worse than making the wrong decision. That applies to life, it applies to business, it applies to everything. It's like sitting in a lake in the middle of the night, stranded, and you don't know which way to row. Well, if you just sit there, you're never gonna get to shore. But if you start rowing and you hit the wrong shore, you'll find out, you can at least turn around and go somewhere else. A lot of people mull about, never pick up the oars – they won't make that decision.'

In addition to being optimistic, they also rarely look back to the past, they seem to be focused and directed to the present and future. Derek Jameson contends that he is a fatalist:

'I go where the wind takes me, I live from day to day. I very rarely think of the past, I don't look backwards and I don't really worry about the future. I just do what's required. Whatever I do today, I must do successfully, as well as I possibly can, and I've got to succeed in everything I do.'

Eddie Shah agrees with this philosophy:

'No point in looking back. I think stress occurs when people try and change their lifestyle, to be something that they are not, that's when stress comes through. Their body must be fighting the change, because the "being of the body" must be saying "Hang on, I don't want to live like this" . . . So what happened yesterday, I've forgotten. I'm only interested in today and tomorrow. That's all I've ever been interested in, and if you asked me what I did last week, I actually have difficulty remembering. I'm very much a get-on-with-it person.'

Many of these stress survivors feel a great deal also depends on hard work, doing the job properly and being a lateral thinker. For example, Victor Kiam feels that success is looking forward and working very hard:

'So when I got out of Harvard Business School, I was really driven. I said, "By golly, I'm going to be just as successful as these people are (those people who had sinecures either because of a family business or parentage of successful corporate executives). But how am I going to make it?" The way I figured it out was to work my tail off, so that's what I did. Today, which is many years later, if you were to say to me, "What do you believe to be success if the bar chart was 100 per cent?", I'd say, "70 per cent is hard work, 20 per cent is brains and ingenuity and 10 per cent is old-fashioned luck." That's to me, what it's all about.'

Working hard is not the only characteristic our stress survivors have in common, but working to the best of their potential. Nicholas Winterton, the Conservative MP for Macclesfield, summed it up succinctly: 'If anything in life is worth doing, it's worth doing properly. That was certainly my attitude toward work when I was working for Ann's father for many years. I mean, if there was something to be done today, it should be done today and not tomorrow.'

And it should be done to the best of your ability without worrying about failure, as Pamela Armstrong emphasizes:

'The thing that I have learnt about more and more in my work, the thing that has liberated me enormously is that I no longer expect total 100 per cent perfection 100 per cent of the time. Occasionally, things go wrong. The world does not stop turning on its axis. Somehow that realization seems to have revitalized me. I do the best I can, given the circumstances, and that seems to have freed me in some ways from worrying too much. I just do the best job I can.'

Sometimes, doing the best job you can may mean seeing solutions in a different light from other people, as Eddie Shah illustrates:

'I have, when I need to, a very devious mind. When I need to, I have the ability to do the Edward de Bono thing, I mean, I have the most lateral mind going. I always look at a problem from another angle, if you come with a difficult problem I will always find another way round it. There was a book about me by two writers, which said that I tend to get the "result of thought" without the "sequence of thought". And it's true, I instinctively come up with the answer.'

In addition to their attitude to work, there are some stress survivors who feel it is tremendously important that individuals attempt to 'sow their oats early in life', to live their dreams before settling for a stable career and family life. It is perhaps not surprising that pop star Rick Wakeman came up with the following advice, given the industry he is in and the crunch events in his life:

'We led, up until our late twenties and early thirties, a pretty outrageous lifestyle, which I'm not condoning, because health-wise it wasn't very clever. I only got away with it because of the business we were in, but we now don't have anything in our lives where we would say "I wish I'd done that!" I'm certain there are a lot of marriages and people who are around who've got their nice family life as we have. But they may have this niggling thing that they wish they'd done one thing or another – gone to America or Australia or gone on safari or anything. I think it is crucial that people can try to, at least, realize one of their dreams or one of their ambitions, and do it before they try and settle into the norm of family life. You must, if you have thousands of dreams, try to realize just one of them, because that will help you tremendously later in life.'

Personality Profile of Our Stress Survivors

It can be seen that our stress survivors are idiosyncratic in nature, possessing a range of unique characteristics. In addition, they have a number of characteristics in common: they seem to possess at least three of the characteristics described by Charles Garfield, in his book *Peak Performers*. First, they tend to perceive themselves as the primary locus of control. Second, they are high in self-mastery, an important element of which is self-confidence, which Garfield described thus: 'Self-confident people feel an internal authority to act, based on a sense of their own expertise and the knowledge that if something goes awry they will know what to do. They count on their capabilities being equal to the task. In short, they trust their own effectiveness.' And finally, they possess what Garfield calls 'ego strength', which is very similar to our hardiness concept:

Ego strength often shows up in business and elsewhere as hardiness – the energy to sustain long hours of work and the flexibility to adapt to change. Hardiness comes from a strong sense of being on course. Less confident coworkers spend significant amounts of their energy hiding behind pronouncements of policy and 'higher authority' and manoeuvring to protect their skins, which tend to be thin.

Our stress survivors may be vulnerable Type As who have had tragic events in their lives, but they have treated these setbacks as 'challenges' to be overcome and 'opportunities for growth'! All in all, they have a positive and optimistic view of life, even under adversity. These are certainly not one of Robert Frost's victims: 'The reason why worry kills more people than work is that more people worry than work.'

4

Life Crunch Points

Research on adult development has illustrated that there are several developmental milestones or life events that are experienced during adulthood. Psychologists such as Erik Erikson have identified young adulthood, middle adulthood and old age as periods during which individuals experience change or 'crises'. Certain life events in adulthood such as leaving home, getting married, becoming a parent or grandparent or retiring are often age-related; however, others such as separation, divorce or death of someone close, can happen at any stage in the life-cycle. Furthermore, the timing of the event in an individual's lifespan is critical to its impact on the person. For example, after being married for some time, being unexpectedly faced with fertility problems was a highly stressful period for Joanna Foster: 'It was the first sort of traumatic life event to hit me, and I had no set coping pattern to fall back on as I'd never had to face such a difficult situation before. Suddenly, life no longer seemed a bed of roses and I realized having children was going to be a major problem. Having children is a major event and for me it was one of life's central expectations. It was eight years before we had our first child.'

Recent theorists such as Daniel Levinson have proposed that not only do individuals experience broad periods of adulthood, but also transition stages. Levinson has identified five eras, each of which contains a series of developmental periods and transitions. These include pre-adulthood (0–22 years); early adulthood (17–45 years); middle adulthood (40–65 years); late adulthood (60 plus years), and late, late adulthood (80 plus years). According to the developmental psychologists Edward Zigler and Matia Finn-Stevenson in their book *Childhood*:

During the stable periods of life, individuals build a life structure by making choices and by striving toward the accomplishment of specific goals. During the transitions, individuals attempt to terminate their existing life structure and initiate a new one, so that they are engaged in reappraising previous choices and goals and moving toward making new ones. Within this sequence of periods and transitions, different life events tend to stand out at different points in the life-cycle.

Consequently, Levinson's theory concentrates not so much on particular life events, but rather on life as it evolves, emphasizing the life structure and the major events such as divorce, bereavement, work and so on. Indeed, this theme of life transitions formed the basis of Gail Sheehy's book *Passages*, in which she wrote: 'Each time we move from one stage of our lives to the next we face a transition, what some have called a "psychosocial crisis" and I have termed a "passage".'

Each of us then must deal with a fairly predictable pattern of passages, events and changes during a lifetime. One's vulnerability to stress can be influenced by events in life which cause undue emotional strain. Simply encountering a significant degree of change, even positive change, in a relatively short period of time, is believed to raise stress levels.

A considerable body of research undertaken in the last fifteen years suggests that life changes are a determining factor in stress-related illnesses. American researchers Holmes and Masuda, at Washington University in St Louis, conducted a survey from which they calculated the relative amounts of 'social adjustment' required after certain life events. They then applied these weightings (that is, evaluations of the degree of seriousness of each life event on a 100-point scale) to the events in the lives of sample populations and arrived at life-change scores for a given period. They found high life-change scores to be related to the onset of illness within the following two-year period. Nevertheless, an important drawback of this type of questionnaire lies in the fact that individual perceptions of the events are not taken into account. Each life event listed in a scale may have a different meaning for each person questioned, but they are rigidly weighted.

The following life stress inventory, designed by Cary and Rachel Cooper, addresses this criticism by incorporating a 10-point rating scale for each life event based on its degree of upset or stressfulness to the individual. Hence, this life stress inventory can help to measure life change and susceptibility to stress-related illness. Although the scale can give some indication of the probability of health breakdown based on the number of simultaneously occurring stressful events, it does not take into account a number of important factors. The extent to which these events lead to ill health will depend to a large degree on a person's capacity to cope with stress, on the personal support the individual has and how important each life event is perceived to be. It can, however, give one an idea of how stress factors, which arise with changes in life, are being experienced by the individual and act as a warning sign for a potentially stressful situation.

Life Events

Place a cross (X) in the 'Yes' column for each event which has taken place in the last two years. Then circle a number on the scale which best describes how upsetting the event crossed was to you, e.g. 10 for death of husband.

Event	Yes	Scale
Bought house		1 2 3 4 5 6 7 8 9 10
Sold house		1 2 3 4 5 6 7 8 9 10
Moved house		1 2 3 4 5 6 7 8 9 10
Major house renovation		1 2 3 4 5 6 7 8 9 10
Separation from loved one		1 2 3 4 5 6 7 8 9 10
End of relationship		1 2 3 4 5 6 7 8 9 10
Got engaged		1 2 3 4 5 6 7 8 9 10
Got married		1 2 3 4 5 6 7 8 9 10
Marital problem		1 2 3 4 5 6 7 8 9 10

Event	Yes	Scale
Awaiting divorce		1 2 3 4 5 6 7 8 9 10
Divorce		1 2 3 4 5 6 7 8 9 10
Child started school/nursery		1 2 3 4 5 6 7 8 9 10
Increased nursing responsibilities for elderly or sick person		1 2 3 4 5 6 7 8 9 10
Problems with relatives		1 2 3 4 5 6 7 8 9 10
Problems with friends/neighbours		1 2 3 4 5 6 7 8 9 10
Pet-related problems		1 2 3 4 5 6 7 8 9 10
Work-related problems		1 2 3 4 5 6 7 8 9 10
Change in nature of work		1 2 3 4 5 6 7 8 9 10
Threat of redundancy		1 2 3 4 5 6 7 8 9 10
Changed job		1 2 3 4 5 6 7 8 9 10
Made redundant		1 2 3 4 5 6 7 8 9 10
Unemployment		1 2 3 4 5 6 7 8 9 10
Retired		1 2 3 4 5 6 7 8 9 10
Increased or new bank loan/mortgage		1 2 3 4 5 6 7 8 9 10
Financial difficulty		1 2 3 4 5 6 7 8 9 10
Insurance problem		1 2 3 4 5 6 7 8 9 10

Event	Yes	Scale
Legal problem		1 2 3 4 5 6 7 8 9 10
Emotional or physical illness of close family or relative		1 2 3 4 5 6 7 8 9 10
Serious illness of close family or relative requiring hospitalization		1 2 3 4 5 6 7 8 9 10
Surgical operation experienced by family member or relative		1 2 3 4 5 6 7 8 9 10
Death of husband		1 2 3 4 5 6 7 8 9 10
Death of family member or relative		1 2 3 4 5 6 7 8 9 10
Death of close friend		1 2 3 4 5 6 7 8 9 10
Emotional or physical illness of yourself		1 2 3 4 5 6 7 8 9 10
Serious illness requiring your own hospitalization		1 2 3 4 5 6 7 8 9 10
Surgical operation on yourself		1 2 3 4 5 6 7 8 9 10
Pregnancy		1 2 3 4 5 6 7 8 9 10
Birth of baby		1 2 3 4 5 6 7 8 9 10
Birth of grandchild		1 2 3 4 5 6 7 8 9 10
Family member left home		1 2 3 4 5 6 7 8 9 10

Event	Yes	Scale
Difficult relationship with children		1 2 3 4 5 6 7 8 9 10
Difficult relationship with parents		1 2 3 4 5 6 7 8 9 10

Plot total score below:

Low stress		High stress
1	50	100

It is important to realize that the amount of change that is taking place in one's life could cause irreparable harm. Changes can arise from factors beyond an individual's control, such as the death of a close relative; other changes one is party to (either willingly or involuntarily), such as divorce, pregnancy and so on.

We were interested in finding out from our stress survivors what they themselves classed as significant life events in their past. In particular, we wanted them to recount those events which could be classed as 'crunch points', in that they actually altered their values and direction and changed their emphasis on what is important in life. Not surprisingly, the most commonly reported crunch points were related to death or illness of someone close, followed by divorce and relationship problems.

Death and Illness

People who have been close to sudden death cannot turn back the clock. They have to discover that life will never be the same again and live with new circumstances. Undoubtedly, one of the most traumatic crunch points must be the death of your own child. This was the turning point for the broadcaster Stuart Hall and it permanently altered his whole philosophy of life and the significance of subsequent life events:

'We had a son, Nicholas, who was born with a hole in his heart. It was a time of enormous stress, coping with a blue baby. He was a beautiful child with beautiful blond hair and blue eyes. We were waiting in those days for an operation to correct narrowed arteries. Today, it would be a routine operation, but then it was unheard of. So that's why I get so angry about people talking about the National Health Service now, when they say, "we need an operation on demand". In those days, there was no such thing as an operation for hole in the heart, and we were told we would have to wait until he was five years old before they could even attempt to operate.

'After three years of constant attention by the doctor, he became seriously ill, so I rang our local GP. He said he would have to be taken to Pendlebury Children's Hospital and wasn't sure whether or not they would have to perform an operation on Nicholas. So I loaded him in my car, with Hazel, my wife, who wrapped him in a blanket. I took him to the hospital and as I was going through Casualty to lay him on the bed, he died. Nicholas died.'

For the musician Rick Wakeman, and broadcasters Jonathan Dimbleby and Gloria Hunniford, the death of their fathers were significant life crunch points: 'When my father died, it was a very traumatic thing for me,' recounted Rick Wakeman. 'I'm no different to anybody else, you realize all the things you wanted to say to your dad, all the things you'd wished you'd never done and wanted to say sorry for. He also died two weeks before his retirement day, and I thought, "What a waste, what a waste of a life" and it was then I suppose that I thought I don't want to waste mine.'

Gloria Hunniford's father was also in show business and as a child he had toured with Gloria giving concerts, which included her performing as a singer. She described the impact of his death nine years ago:

'The really, really big hurdle for me was when my father died. I had been unusually close to this man, and we had a relationship which was very much on a friend basis. He was self-educated, very bright and could turn his hand to anything and I

mean anything, whether it was painting, poetry, manual stuff –
he was a great man to look up to and a great father.

'He had a stroke, and really, the dad I knew went at that
particular point. He lived about another four years after the
first one, and he had another couple of minor ones. Really, that
first one was the big blow in that he was so healthy and fit
before, and you just think your parents are going to go on for
ever. He was quite young, as he was only in his early sixties, so
it wasn't on the cards, he'd never had a day's illness before that.
So suddenly, when we got a phone call in the middle of the
night to say he had had this stroke and was in hospital, I mean
that was devastation. My reaction was, well absolutely crushed
of course, but I think that when I saw him, I felt totally helpless.
I suppose that after growing up with this bright, bubbly sort of
person and then when you actually see somebody "diminished
of life" like that; well, it's terribly emotional to talk about. I
think the hardest realization with the death of parents – and the
same thing happened to my mother who died a year ago – is
knowing somebody so well all your life, and suddenly they're no
longer there. When I first heard that my mother had got cancer,
once again I had this glow in my stomach, this gut reaction and
that feeling that the whole bottom of your world has dropped
out again.'

In fact, the death of someone close often enhances a feeling
of loss of control. Individuals often thought they knew where
they were going and what was going to happen to them, they
thought they could plan the future. Then suddenly, they receive
this signal which tells them they have no control over their life.

The death of Richard Dimbleby had such a profound effect
on his son Jonathan that he wrote a book about it:

'The first major stress in my life was his dying. The effect on
me was a perpetual pain, it doesn't go away and it was, in a
sense, the feeling of being robbed at just the worst moment in
one's life. I was twenty-one but I was reaching the stage where I
thought that, "I can show them what I can do." Then after that
there's the permanent regrets – something which I think is true
of anyone whose father dies when they're young – things like
"He's missing ever seeing my children," and so on.

'He died of cancer. It was a long illness, as he had cancer for about five years, and he bore it with extraordinary status. We knew about it from the beginning. He made the decision to tell us. I remember it very clearly, it was in 1960 and I was sixteen. It was very upsetting for all of us and yet you believed that he would conquer it, that he wouldn't die. He did not seem like someone who was likely to die, as he had a big solid existence.

'He was extraordinary about it and was able to talk about it openly. I wrote a book about it, and how he handled it very much affects my own judgements today. It was perturbing, alarming and shocking, as cancer meant a death sentence then. It wasn't anything you usually talked about, it was not a disease to be mentioned. In fact, although the family knew, we didn't tell anyone else and the BBC for instance didn't know. There were the odd rumours of course, but no one in fact knew for certain. He would go and have treatment at St Thomas's Hospital on Monday morning and do the television programme *Panorama* on Monday night. He obviously had remissions, but during that five-year period, he carried on working completely normally, until about three months before he died.'

When we interviewed Elizabeth Emanuel and David Emanuel (formerly 'The Emanuels' prior to their separation), David was still recovering from the shock of his mother's sudden death a couple of weeks earlier:

'The funeral was on Friday. The situation was that she'd had a brain haemorrhage and she was in hospital. I knew that she wasn't going to pull through. It was such a shock because she was such a strong and healthy person and had so much energy, and had so much good to give that my immediate reaction was that I just couldn't cope. I just let it all come out. I just cried and cried. Then on the day of the funeral there was nothing left, it was all gone, I didn't feel anything. Whereas some of my brothers who'd previously shown no emotion, at the funeral it all came out. I kept thinking – you've got to control it. I just felt empty on the day, but then I thought, "If we all break down, how is my father going to cope?"

'It's going to affect me in lots of ways. I'll think, "Come showtime now, it'll just be my father coming up," which will be strange, because my mother loved coming up to see what Elizabeth and I were working on, whereas my father's not particularly interested. It's bound to be different and when I go down to Wales and when we take the children down, it will be different because my mother won't be there too. I've still got a lot of adjustments and grieving to do.'

For some of the older personalities we interviewed, illness and the death of someone close of a similar age reminded them of their own mortality. Victor Kiam described the effect a terminal illness of a close friend had had on him, and then continued about being aware of his own vulnerability:

'I'm very, very lucky (touch wood). I'd say to myself, I'm the Iron Duke and nothing is going to happen because nothing had happened. However, when I got a detached retina, I woke up with it, I wasn't in an accident or anything, it just happened. All of a sudden, you get a sense of your own vulnerability. I still think of myself as twenty-one years old and that I can do everything I could do when I was twenty-one – but you can't keep it up, can you?'

Fortunately, Eddie Shah's wife made a miraculous recovery from cervical cancer but this proved to be his major crunch point, and it changed the whole direction of his life:

'Until about six years ago, I was a drifter, I don't mean I was scared to do anything, but I was drifting. Then my wife got cancer. She was in Christies, and was given four months to live. We had three children. She had radiotherapy, an operation and then went on to chemotherapy after that. This is when a lot of stress happened. I remember, I rang my dad the night I found out she'd got it. All I said was "Hi, dad" and he said "Hi" to me, and then I just started to cry and I must have cried for about five minutes. It must have been awful for him when you think about it, he knew something had happened but he couldn't even find out what it was! Anyway, although I do get emotional, I think that's the first time something has ever really come out.

'I remember one particular day when she was ill in hospital, it was 9 December 1982 and her temperature was very up and down. It was about 103 or 104, or whatever the maximum is before you blow up and there'd be sort of fans on her, all the clothes were off her and I washed round her. Then, half an hour later her temperature had dropped right down and they had blankets on her and hot water bottles. This just went on and on for about half a day. I remember the guy who did the operation saying to me, "I've got to say, I don't think she's going to make it today." But she did. And, touch wood, she's around today giving me hell and doing very well. She's fine but she's the first person to beat that strain of cancer.

'But that day in 1982 I saw somebody faced with life and death, not grey, just life with death, black and white – that's it. And since that point on, life's been very easy for her, because the value of life suddenly became very important. And that's when you realize you've got to do things for yourself. And therefore, all the sorts of things such as wanting to have a lot of money and all the peripheral thoughts I'd had up until that point about why I wanted to work, why I wanted to be successful – just ceased to be important.'

Divorce

Like death, divorce, separation and affairs are linked with a whole host of feelings ranging from loss to failure and guilt. Without exception, all our interviewees who had been through a relationship trauma isolated the event as being one of great stress which often resulted in stress-related illness or behaviour. Publishing executive Helen Fraser, for example, ended up needing psychotherapy, while the poet and writer Roger McGough retreated to his bed.

'I was in psychotherapy for about seven years from about twenty-five to my early thirties,' recalled Helen Fraser. 'It was mainly triggered off by the whole business of getting involved with Grant [her present husband] who was then married. It was all very difficult and there didn't seem to be any solution, any way out. Anyway, in the end, his marriage did break up and he also went into therapy with the same person, but separately.

'I think the therapy was fantastically useful because, for a start, I am sure we would never have stayed together because most "exit relationships from marriage" are doomed. You know, you are just the path for someone to leave their marriage.'

The break-up of Roger McGough's first marriage was exacerbated by a number of other negative life events which were happening simultaneously:

'I started going out with my first wife in my late twenties and we were together about ten years. It was stressful being in a relationship when you wanted to be somewhere else, but there's so many things that keep you there, the children and all those things. You can never get out of it. It was common sense to break up and get a divorce, but we carried on and on and on, and that was the worst part.

'Eventually, we did separate, culminating in divorce over a period of five years. That was a very stressful time. Things were awkward, it was difficult, you had to cope with the day-to-day things. I was working very hard anyway, my mother was ill and dying, the children were taken from me – all the things which lead to stress. Probably, it showed in me by drinking heavily, and I also used to spend a lot of time in bed. I also wrote about it in *Holiday on Death Row*, there was always a need to write all the time. I reckon writing about my experience probably helped me in a sense, as a focus for my misery. In fact, I wrote a poem which refers to my habit of taking to my bed when depressed.'

Depressed?

When you're
depressed
deep rest
is best.

(*Nailing the Shadow*,
1987, Viking Press)

For the politician Austin Mitchell, the break-up of his marriage was the first real time he had ever had to deal with personal emotional turmoil:

'I returned to Britain in 1963 and found it had changed, and was much more exciting. I also had an affair with Linda [his present wife], as a result of which I got divorced. That involved the pressures of fear of discovery, being found out and that caused torments. It was the first emotional testing I'd ever had, everything had been straightforward up until then. Getting a divorce was a really tough time emotionally. I can't remember it having any great ill effects upon me, apart from occasionally getting knotted up. I think the main effect was just a feeling of guilt, but the main problem was having the responsibility of letting everyone down in that kind of fashion.

'The main thing that I find causes stress is personal relationships and emotional problems rather than career problems, so doing a difficult job or speaking to an audience, well that's fairly straightforward in comparison.'

Derek Jameson viewed the break-up of his marriages as great failures in his life and attributed it largely to his own deprived upbringing. In fact, he was so afraid of continually repeating the same pattern, that he was with his third wife for eleven years before actually 'tying the knot':

'It causes me great regret and pain that the two marriages ended disastrously – I'm not happy with that situation at all. I put it down as a great failure in my life that I was unable to sustain a proper, normal family relationship. I think it's because I never had a family relationship as a child. What most people regard as the norm, for me has always been the abnorm – marriage, families, husbands, wives and all that, had never really figured in my life in those early years, so I'm not very good at them – I'm much better doing my own thing.'

Ironically, he admits that the Jewish culture and its emphasis on the importance of the family was one of the attractions in his marriage to his first wife: 'As far as I know, my father was a Jew, that's why I was in the children's home because I was the classic product of a relationship between a Shiksa and a Jewish lad in the days when it was impossible. They'd never have married as it was just unheard of for a Jew to marry out of his or her religion.

'So, knowing I had this Jewish blood, I went through a Jewish phase when I attached myself to my first wife and to a big, warm, cosy Jewish family, all living at the top of their voices. I leapt on to it like a man seizing at something great and wonderful. I'd never ever known this kind of situation with brothers, sisters, aunts and uncles.

'But, it all ended disastrously, and we finally divorced. As a wife and mother, she was very unstable, and was in and out of mental hospitals for much of our married life. She was classified as a manic depressive, but she always thought that there was something wrong organically with her head. However, the psychiatrist said "no", it was purely neurosis, probably caused by her parents battling against each other when she was a kid. Then she dropped dead one day with a massive brain haemorrhage, which of course raises the question – was she right, was there something organically wrong with her after all?

'I'd left her by that time and gone to Manchester, and had various relationships. However, I've always stayed close to my children and there was never any problem there. Then I married a Manchester girl in the early seventies, and we had two children but that marriage ended in divorce, because I came back to London and got involved with a girl in London. I still live with her now and she's my manager. We got married recently after eleven years and I made sure I didn't rush into it this time. Third time round, I think I've learnt by my mistakes!'

New Environments

Several of our personalities pinpointed a number of stressful life events associated with having to adapt to new living environments. Linda Kelsey, the magazine editor, found leaving home at seventeen to go to university was a very frightening experience:

'I was shy and scared, really scared, and I found the work hard to understand, because I had been very good at learning by rote. My way of dealing with not being able to cope with the work was to escape from it, and not attend any lectures and hardly do any essays – and, disappear basically. It's extraordinary, you can disappear and nobody notices. Nobody comes after you and says "You're a naughty girl, why don't you come along?", which is what would happen at school.

'Also, life creates an escape route, because I found myself a boyfriend very quickly, and sort of got involved in other things and actually had a very nice time for a year. Then, at the end of the year, I failed one of three exams. I managed in the end to pass two but it was hell and instead of going back to resit it, I dropped out. Even that was quite stressful as well in a way.'

Leaving home to go into the Army was an unpleasant time for Stuart Hall: 'I had to go into the Army and it was very stressful, everyone piled into the same hut. I had never mixed with criminals before. It was a whole assortment of people, Cambridge and Oxford graduates and this bunch from Scotland who were the dregs of humanity. We went through hell for six weeks. These thugs stole all our kit, all our money. We were too terrified to ask for it back, as it was pointless to reason with these guys.'

Sir Terence Conran recalled a traumatic episode when he was a schoolboy, although he tends to use this as a vehicle for exploring more abstract concepts:

'I was shot at while walking down a country lane by a rear gunner in a German bomber. I think it's about the only thing that I can think of that has been traumatic. Trauma, I believe, is only the experience you have at birth. You can't ever experience anything other than trauma at birth, maybe death is also trauma – I don't know.'

Moving house is commonly noted as one of the most stressful life events, and broadcaster Pamela Armstrong viewed her recent house purchase as something which exceeded any of the stress she has to cope with at work: 'For me, a stressful situation is something like buying or moving house. It's quite different from anything I've ever experienced in my professional life. It was intolerable stress over which I had no control. It didn't seem to affect me physically, it was just a constantly gnawing pressure.'

You're Fired!

Although almost all of the life crunch points and stressful life events isolated by our 'stress survivors' were non-work-related, at least two personalities described their shock reactions to suddenly being sacked – an act of punishment and rejection. When Austin Mitchell was dismissed from the Labour Party's Shadow Cabinet for accepting a job as presenter of a Sky Television programme, he was both surprised and dismayed:

'I was upset by being fired by Neil Kinnock, because it

seemed to be a very easy and straightforward job I'd been offered, which I could combine with politics, doing a political programme for Sky Television, which I quite liked. I didn't see why there should have been any problem and indeed, when they rang up and said would I do this and would I do that, I said "yes", as it sounded a good idea. I thought it would be interesting and (a) the money is always useful and (b) it's nice to be in a studio and (c) there's always the interesting way of plotting through someone's mind and grappling with an issue when you're interviewing. Incidentally, since then others have been allowed to do similar programmes and stay on the front bench.

'I just thought I would see if I could do it and that there would be no problem, I didn't even bother to ask about it. I was therefore surprised when Kinnock said "it's incompatible". It wasn't that I was conscious of what I was doing, I was offered the job and considered it like every other job that I get offered, and decided to accept.'

When Helen Fraser was fired from her publishing job after eleven years, initially she was shattered, although in the long term it proved to be beneficial as far as her career was concerned:

'There was a frightful political row and I was booted out. It was a very shattering experience for me and I had three months chewing the carpet and wishing to destroy everyone who'd done this to me, and then I felt OK again. It's funny because most of the time I was fine, I mean, after the initial period, but every now and then the misery would return. I'd be cleaning the bath or something and then be absolutely overwhelmed with rage and misery and sob and sob. And Grant would say, "Well, come on, what's the matter?" And I'd say, "Well you know, I don't think they've suffered enough." He'd reply, "Of course they've suffered. They've had to pay you a fortune, they're getting terrible publicity, it's been fantastically damaging – what more do you want?"

'When I was with the other publishing company, I was always being offered other jobs and I would always think "better the devil you know". I was very happy and I would never have left because I built myself a cosy little box and I thought "within these walls, I'm safe, I know what I'm doing, there are no challenges I can't cope with". But, at the same time, if I look back on it, actually I was beginning to get bored precisely because there were no challenges. So when, after twenty-one job offers, I came to Heinemann, it was absolutely terrifying for a bit, it was the best possible thing that could have happened to me, to be suddenly pushed into a management role. All at once you have thirty or forty people whose lives you are responsible for, you have to produce a certain amount of turnover and a certain amount of profit. I've found that given those challenges, I could rise to them and it wasn't impossible.'

For both Austin Mitchell and Helen Fraser, going through the humiliation of being sacked was enhanced by the blaze of publicity it attracted. None the less, like all our stress survivors, they both survived the stress and, in fact, redirected a potentially negative life event into a positive one.

Our Pathfinders

In her more recent book, *Pathfinders*, Gail Sheehy identified a specific type of individual she labelled as a pathfinder. These were people who

by successfully navigating through a passage or emerging victorious from a life accident, know what strengths they can count on when under fire. They demonstrate important qualities – quite apart from basic mood, social style and energy level – that are shaped by life experience and enable them to attempt further development, leaps or to withstand a life accident.

From our analysis of the ways in which our stress survivors handled the 'crunch points' in their lives, undoubtedly all of them qualified to join the rank of pathfinder. By far the greatest stressful life events involved those which precipitated mourning, particularly death of someone dear. However, even tragic experiences such as these can ultimately be transcended. According to Gail Sheehy:

Transcendence is a realm beyond all the negative emotions of mourning, beyond even the neutral point of acceptance. When it happens that a life accident creates a pathfinder, the person is able to transcend his former self as well. A positive self-fulfilling prophecy is made as one comes out of the dark hours. And around a new work, idea, purpose, faith, or a love inspired by the accident, one's goals are realigned. Transcendence is an act of creativity. One creates a partial replacement for what has been lost. The light at the end of mourning is glimpsed and it is cause for new joys.

5

Divided Loyalties

In addition to personal crunch points and life events, home-life stress is dependent upon an extremely complicated series of factors, some of which are illustrated in Table 4. Surprisingly little research has been carried out to identify the major stress agents which spill over from work to family and vice versa. Nevertheless, it is commonly recognized that these exist and can adversely affect our mental and physical well-being.

In their book *Must Success Cost So Much?*, Paul Evans and Fernando Bartolomé categorized five different patterns of relationship that exist between one's work and non-work experiences: (1) spill-over – 'one affects the other, in a positive or negative way'; (2) independence – 'they exist side by side and for all practical purposes are independent of each other'; (3) conflict – 'they are in conflict with each other and cannot be easily reconciled'; (4) instrumentality – 'one is primarily a means of obtaining something derived in the other'; and (5) compensation – 'one is a way of making up for what is missing in the other'. These authors found that the experience of spill-over, sometimes in conjunction with any one other pattern, was the most common relationship in the successful managers they studied.

In his novel, *Nice Work*, David Lodge humorously portrays his managing director, Vic Wilcox, as typifying a mixture of negative spill-over and compensation:

At about the same time that evening, Vic Wilcox was restively watching television with his younger son, Gary, in the lounge of the five-bedroomed, four-lavatoried, neo-Georgian house on Avondale Road. Marjorie was upstairs in bed, reading *Enjoy Your Menopause*, or, more likely, had already fallen asleep over it. Raymond was out boozing somewhere with his cronies and Sandra was at a disco with the spotty Cliff. Gary was too young to go out on a Saturday night and Vic was . . . not too old, of course, but disinclined . . . When he worked for Vanguard, he and Marjorie had belonged to a rather gay crowd of other young managers and their wives, who used to meet regularly in each other's houses on Saturday nights; but it turned out that there was a lot of hanky-panky going on at those parties, or after them, or in between them and the circle eventually broke up in an atmosphere of scandal and recrimination. Since those days, Vic had moved on and up the career ladder to a point where he seemed to have no friends any more, only business acquaintances and all social life was an extension of work.

Taking a somewhat more serious approach, we were interested in finding out from our stress survivors just how they had managed the delicate balancing act involved in dividing loyalties between work and home pressures.

Table 4: Life Stress at Home

The need to succeed
Constant push and drive generated by self, partner, parents, organizations towards successful career, financial and status circumstances.

Partner relationships
Conflicts of home and work life, struggling to maintain relationships amidst the changing roles of men and women.

Relationships with children
Conflict of time spent with children, work- and home-life pressures, concern over their health and education and responsibility for their future.

Personal circumstances and life events
The unexpected traumatic event, or constant aggravation of personal circumstances such as divorce, single parenthood, financial insecurity, etc.

The Need to Succeed

Commitment beyond normal working hours is expected by many companies, and is a common trait found in highly ambitious individuals – which most of our interviewees certainly were. This can involve the need to bring work home, attending meetings and conferences, as well as social entertaining. Certainly this can have beneficial career effects, but at a cost. Indeed, Joseph Heller, in his book *Something Happened*, highlights this phenomenon in terms of his organizational Happiness Charts:

At the very top [of the Happiness Charts], of course, are those people, mostly young and without dependants, to whom the company is not yet an institution of any sacred merit (or even an institution especially worth preserving) but still only a place to work and who regard their present association with it as something temporary. To them, it's all just a job, from President to partner and pretty much the same job at that . . . Near the bottom of my Happiness Charts I put those people who are striving so hard to get to the top.

Most studies have shown that top executives work very long hours. In their book *High Flyers*, for example, Charles Cox and Cary Cooper discovered that chief executives in UK organizations accepted long work hours and heavy schedules of travel as a necessary part of life. Even so, there were some expressions of guilt that perhaps they did not spend enough time with their families and, particularly, that this lifestyle had placed an undue burden of responsibility on their wives for maintenance of the home and for bringing up the children.

We also found in our assessment of the stress survivors that the majority of them had worked long hours that intruded into their family life, particularly earlier on in their careers. Moreover, some personalities such as Derek Jameson still looked back on this with great regret: 'If anyone asked me to categorize what had gone wrong in my life, I'd say that I never ever devoted enough time to my family. I was always too busy with my career, with my obsessional drive to get to the top, to succeed in newspapers, in the work I was doing.'

The long hours demanded by the newspaper business were also mentioned by Eddie Shah: 'I remember the time when I was stuck working *away* from my family in London, I once didn't see them for seven weeks. I can tell you, it was a hard seven weeks as I didn't have any family support. They didn't come down to see me and I didn't go up. It was a seven-day newspaper, it was relentless.'

The life of a politician is also renowned for unsocial working hours and long periods away from home. Nicholas Winterton described his early days on his way up the political ladder as being a time when his 'visits' home were infrequent, to say the least:

'While still working at a full-time job, I also got involved in a trade professional association – Contract Mechanical Engineers in the Midlands. It was one of the biggest branches nationally and I became their youngest ever chairman. I was devoting a great deal of time and often I wouldn't return home until half past eight or even nine o'clock in the evening. Sometimes, if there were business meetings it wouldn't be until twelve o'clock or half past midnight, and Ann would by then be in bed asleep. Then I got into local government, and before long my energies were directed elsewhere, and I went into local politics where I devoted a tremendous amount of time. I sat on about forty-odd committees and my attendance record was over 90 per cent.'

His wife Ann Winterton interrupted the conversation at this point: 'In fact, the joke went round the county council that our daughter was conceived on the only night in the year that Nicholas didn't have a meeting!' 'That's something I'm *not* going to comment on,' retorted Nicholas.

In their book *Reluctant Managers – Their Work and Life Style*, Richard Scase and Robert Goffee found that it was the senior managers who were more likely to find that preoccupations with work affected their private lives. Furthermore, the higher up the organizational hierarchy they climbed, the harder they found it to separate the two worlds of work and home. Once again, David Lodge's central character in *Nice Work* typifies this sort of spill-over:

Victor Wilcox lies awake, in the dark bedroom, waiting for his quartz alarm clock to bleep. It is set to do this at 6.45. How long he has to wait he doesn't know. He could easily find out by groping for the clock, lifting it to his line of vision and pressing the button that illuminates the digital display. But he would rather not know. Supposing it is only six o'clock? Or even five? It could be five. Whatever it is, he won't be able to get to sleep again. This had become a regular occurrence lately: lying awake in the dark, waiting for the alarm to bleep, worrying.

Worries streak towards him like enemy spaceships in one of Gary's video games. He flinches, dodges, zaps them with instant solutions, but the assault is endless: the Avco account, the Rawlinson account, the price of pig-iron, the value of the pound, the competition from Foundrax, the incompetence of his Marketing Director, the persistent breakdowns of the core blowers, the vandalising of the toilets in the fettling shop, the pressure from his divisional boss, last month's accounts, the quarterly forecast, the annual review . . .

Being Controller of BBC1 TV means that Jonathan Powell is always 'on call' should any emergency arise – indeed, he admits to having several televisions often on at the same time at home: 'In this job, the work carries over into home and social life because you're watching television a lot and you're always "on call". If something happens such as the Lockerbie disaster, everyone has to know where you are. In cases like that, the schedule has to be changed and people have to make decisions about whether to put the news in, what to try and so on.'

Again, because of the specific nature of their profession, David Emanuel and Elizabeth Emanuel said that even when they went out together for a social night out they often found it difficult to switch off from work because they often bumped into clients. 'When we go to concerts in London, for example, we always tend to see people we know through work, so it ends up being a cross between a social and a work outing – it's not really cutting off, is it?' asked David.

However, there were a few individuals, such as Pamela Armstrong, who even from an early stage in her broadcasting career had managed to compartmentalize work and home stressors and avoid any spill-over:

'I never take work home with me, when I come home work is really forgotten. I think that this is probably an important thing although it's not something I've consciously cultivated, because I feel it's healthy, it's just the way I've always been. When I'm at home, I'm not interested in my working life; and when I'm working, I have little recollection and speak very little about my home life. I simply become immersed in whatever surrounds me – it's just the way I am.'

Partner Relationships

Social support is an important factor buffering the impact of stressful experiences and many of our stress survivors emphasized the important role their partners had played in this respect. The ultimate opportunity for understanding, support and being colleagues occurs when husband and wife are in the same profession. Nevertheless, as Ann Winterton pointed out, there may also be disadvantages:

'When I first followed Nicholas into politics, we both perceived there was a problem, as I wasn't pushing myself forward enough and people were turning to Nicholas to talk to rather than addressing me. So Nick refused to accompany me on business unless he was specifically asked, and that was absolutely great for over a year. Now he's beginning to join me and, of course, they're loving it, but I'm very much number one in my own constituency. They chose me, knowing that Nicholas was in the House.'

In fact, her husband believed that following in his footsteps, career-wise, had actually helped cement a better understanding between them in relation to the demands of the job:

'I think that it's actually been quite helpful, Ann coming into Parliament, because she now knows the pressures under which I was operating and, in the past, would never actually believe it. She now realizes that the sort of decisions I was having to make all along were justified, decisions which, from time to time, she had felt were unnecessary. To an extent then there's been a countervailing benefit by her joining me in the House, as far as I'm concerned.'

Being able to discuss work pressures with her former business partner, David Emanuel, was viewed by Elizabeth Emanuel as being essential:

'It's good to have a partner because you can "off-load" the stressors. Also I find that if you share things that bother you, you don't have to bottle them inside. I have been to a psychoanalyst in the past, but the only problem with that is that you have to devote a certain amount of time, time which I just don't have at the moment. I know friends who go and then say that it's a tremendous relief, because you can just get it all out of your system. That's if you don't have somebody you can talk to.'

Rick Wakeman's wife Nina Carter was also in the rock music business and was a former member of the band Blonde on Blonde. She was also a highly successful model and, like her husband, acknowledges that their mutual support was the main saving grace in their previously highly turbulent and often self-destructive lives:

'We were very lucky because we both had been very ambitious and were both quite progressive people – we have forced each other forward in lots of ways and we've supported each other greatly. In everything I do, Rick's always there behind me and I like to think I do the same thing for him. I think as far as married couples are concerned, it's very important to do as much as possible together and even if you have children, to remember that when your children leave home, you still have each other.'

Rick Wakeman went further and maintained that Nina's support had actually saved his life:

'If I hadn't met Nina, I probably wouldn't be here talking to you now, and that's not a flippant statement. Something drastic would have happened. At some stage, a doctor would have told me to stop drinking, and then it would have been very much a matter of whether or not life was worth stopping drinking for, or whether the drinking was more important.

'You've got to have something to work for in life, a bit of encouragement. I often think it would be interesting if they put a drug addict who was on the same level as an alcoholic to work together to solve their problems, rather than two alcoholics together or two drug addicts together, because I think the things run parallel but they're not the same – you're not competing any more. That was the great thing, we weren't competing and we were helping each other. I have to be brutally honest, and I don't think it's being far-fetched to say that if it hadn't been for Nina, I'd probably be dead.'

Magazine editor Linda Kelsey, like many career women, waited until her late thirties to have her first child. As a working mother, she believes her partner's supportiveness has been crucial, although she is well aware of the negative effects the demands of their lifestyle could have on their relationship:

'I must have reached a point in my life around the time I met Christian about five years ago, when I realized that nice men aren't boring. If you find a nice man, grab him, because you can have a fantastic and difficult time with men, but in the long run, if you have a career and then go on to have a baby, you need a supportive partner. I just couldn't handle it now, if I had a really difficult man who was non-supportive – that would probably be when I would crack, if I was going to at any time.

'Nevertheless, I'm not pretending it's easy. If you're still at that stage when you're in love with somebody and you want to be with them, to spend time talking to them, in reality snatching time together when you work and have a baby, is really hard. However, I think you can override that in the long term, if you've got a very strong relationship. I can see that you have to be so aware and so watchful, and it's easy to understand how as a couple you could drift apart. You both go to work and you both have a baby, but as far as the two of you coming together is concerned – it could disappear altogether.'

For some dual-career couples, it is not always possible to reach an acceptable solution which enables them to fulfil both partners' career needs and to live together. Commuter marriages are becoming more common and, in their recent book *Career Couples*, Suzan Lewis and Cary Cooper highlighted that living apart can threaten the sense of what marriage should be, and diminish each partner's sense of security. Individuals may feel depressed, lonely or resentful about each other's independence. Often a period of adjustment is necessary when partners do have time together. On the positive side, it can increase the romantic attachment of husbands and wives, equalize the division of labour and open new horizons for career advancement. Even so, overall, it tends to be a forced choice, the benefits of which often outweigh the costs only in specific situations.

After living abroad for ten years because of her husband's job, Joanna Foster and her husband returned to London where she successfully launched the Pepperell Unit at the Industrial Society. Shortly afterwards, they were faced with the dilemma of Jerome being offered the 'perfect job' in France again. They opted for a commuter marriage, the pitfalls and benefits of which are described by Joanna:

'It was a very major crisis for us, really, because I had also recently had a hysterectomy and we had just converted our new house, having been gazumped on five previous houses. So the very idea that we might have to uproot and move back to France was not on the cards. It seemed to me, moving back to France would be a backward move career-wise, and yet it was a perfect job being offered to Jerome. So it took a lot of talking through and I felt very, very emotional about the whole thing. However, it was quite clear that we [the family] should all stay put and Jerome would do the commuting.

'It was a very difficult time as I'd envisaged us living happily ever after in Oxford, and I was into a work project which was incredibly important, building up the Pepperell Unit and loving it, even though it was terribly hard work. So, suddenly, the very idea of taking on anything else to rock the boat even more, was almost more than I could bear. The fact that I was going to have to do the "single parent" bit during the week, as well as coping with an enormous job, and then have to concentrate on our life as a couple at the weekends, seemed an enormous wrench. I didn't feel I actually had the energy to cope with it. In fact, all the flak came not from Jerome and the children but from other members of my family, about God and what he said about marriage and all that stuff.

'Nevertheless, some really good things came out of what was a very difficult situation initially. Jerome came home at weekends, and it took us some time to work out that the Friday night was not a good time to air problems, as everybody was tired and bad-tempered and not in a fit state to deal with them. We learnt to sleep on them and start really talking things out on the Saturday.

'It lasted three years and it was only really when it stopped, that we realized what it had involved and how we'd worked out a really good routine. The very good thing that it put into focus for both of us, was that we really learnt how to use our weekends very positively. We carefully planned ways of recharging our batteries, both as a family and a couple, as well as individuals.'

Relationships with Children

Most of the women we interviewed had not taken career breaks after they had had children. An exception was the politician Ann Winterton who reflected that her time at home looking after young children while her husband's career flourished was fairly bleak: 'Personally, it was one of the worst periods of my life, because the children were young and it was a great strain having to cope on your own. Nicholas was very involved with his job, quite rightly so too, making a tremendous reputation for himself, but it was very difficult for me.'

In our book *Stress and the Woman Manager*, we found that professional women working full-time and with children (especially young children at home) had to spend more time with their children than male managers do, find themselves less able to relax at the end of the day and are even more susceptible to feelings of guilt, role conflict, work overload, tiredness and ill health. Research indicates that for men the work role is often allowed to intrude into the family (e.g., dinner delayed because of a meeting), whereas for women the family role is commonly allowed to intrude on the work role (e.g., leaving work early to take care of a sick child). Consequently, this reverse order of intrusion for the sexes often places additional pressure on working mothers. Even with a supportive partner, Linda Kelsey typified a woman faced with these new motherhood stressors:

'Currently, my main pressure points stem from the amount of things I have to do in my life . . . the work overload and trying to get a decent balance between work and home. Whereas, in fact, there is no decent balance, so you just have to compromise. At the moment, there's a bit less happening in terms of what I'm giving to my work, not so much in hours, but rather I feel I'm still trying to get back that sort of creative spark that was there before I had the baby. It's sort of there, but there's a little bit of my brain somewhere else. Then, when I'm at home with the baby, I feel I need to give him all my time. I'm up with him at five-thirty or six when he wakes in the morning, and stay with him until I have to rush into the shower and get ready to come to work. Then, when I get home in the evening, I literally bolt through the door, drop whatever I'm holding, my coat or whatever, and hold him until he's fast asleep.'

The overload demands stemming from being a full-time mother and having a full-time job often caused the author Bel Mooney to have sleepless nights:

'I suppose the situation I'm in could be described as being high stress, and I would say it was a classic situation for a lot of women like me. I've just taken on a big writing project which involves a lot of research and travels abroad. I have two children, one who's ten and who needs me all the time. I don't have a nanny or a mother's help. I also have a sixteen-year-old boy, who I'm trying to coach for his GCSEs which are very imminent – which is worrying me and him. At the same time, and this is probably the straw that breaks the camel's back, my daughter needs a Victorian dress made for her school play. So, this is the situation I'm in and I'm wondering how I'm going to cope. I will cope, but it still keeps me awake at night.'

Work overload like this also results in lack of relaxation and leisure time. The married television presenters Richard Madeley and Judy Finnigan have four children, including two under school age.

'I would love some space in the day when we weren't always surrounded by demands,' said Judy. 'We have to make sure we get home by five, as our nanny starts very early at seven and as soon as we hit the door, she's off. That's fine, but we then take over at possibly the most stressful period because by tea time, they're all exhausted, tired and cross.

'We then get the babies to bed before seven, because they're awake before six in the morning. The two older ones, meanwhile, go upstairs to watch television because they know the babies will scream and spoil it for them if they stay downstairs.'

Richard continued: 'Once the babies are asleep, we sit down and pour ourselves a drink. Then you hear this bump, bump, bump and the older twins are down and we say, "Boys, please, five minutes, just give us five minutes." So, the stress is dealing with all of that and the children's needs and problems, their homework and so on. Then, they get to bed for about nine and because we're up in the morning at six o'clock, we go to bed by ten at the latest. Judy often goes to bed at the same time as the boys.'

All the stress survivors we talked to with young children complained of tiredness and a desperate need for more uninterrupted sleep. For example, Judy Finnigan complained:

'I find that I get panicky because I know I need a lot of sleep, as I have to be up by six and I know the babies may wake me in the night. Occasionally, I find myself lying in bed unable to sleep, but usually I fall straight off because I'm totally knackered. Often though, I find I wake up at about two o'clock in the morning and then I start worrying, oh god, I've got to be up in about four hours. For example, last night the baby had chicken pox, so she was very miserable and not at all well. She was awake several times in the night and we were up at six. Lack of sleep is a major stress point for me and I can't function properly without it. We have to be firing on full cylinders by seven o'clock. We drive to the studio and while Richard drives, I go through my briefs or interview scripts and we discuss things that are coming up in the show. We arrive at work at eight, then I go straight into make-up and it's straight into doing a live television programme. It's hard if you've had a bad night and my mind is also full of the programme. I feel really uptight about it, because I think children crying is one of the most stressful things in the world.'

Like Judy, Linda Kelsey returned to work shortly after her baby was born:

'I was incredibly tired at the beginning, when I came back to work when Thomas was three months old. But now that he's sleeping through the night, and even though I certainly get less sleep than I used to, I've sort of adapted to it. Sometimes though, I almost talk myself into feeling desperately tired because I think I must be. At weekends, Christian and I do a bit of shift work and I'll go back to sleep for an hour or two and he'll get up, and vice versa.'

Interestingly, when David and Elizabeth Emanuel were married and working together, they also adopted a shift childcare system to enable both of them space and time-out from parenthood as well as from each other.

'We take turns to have separate weekends away, because we're with each other all week and we've found that really beneficial,' said Elizabeth. 'David will have the children one weekend, and I'll have them another weekend and one or other of us will just go off and relax somewhere. I recently went to Champneys, and I think that it's vitally important to keep some system like that working.'

Inevitably, well-known personalities are also faced with the additional pressures of being recognized in public and always 'being on show', even in their parenting roles. Judy Finnigan viewed this aspect of success as particularly stressful:

'I love presenting on television, I really do enjoy it and if it's confined to the show, then that's fine. However, increasingly, I feel we're giving a performance the whole bloody time, even when we go shopping. Everybody knows we present *This Morning* as a couple, and that we're married and it's a very up front family, and our kids are typecast and all the rest of it. You sort of feel that every time you go out, you've got to be this perfect smiling, happy family.'

Richard agreed and continued: 'It's not that it's a problem needing a solution, I think it's just one of those things you have to accept. I think you're overcome by events. I mean, if a three-year-old is actually freaking out and throwing ice cubes around the pub and you say, "Do that one more time and I'm really going to smack you," then he does it again and you whack him, then people go "Oh and I thought they did a piece on the telly last week about not smacking children – well fancy that!" But the kid needed a whack, so you gave him one.'

In *Superwoman*, in the section dealing with how to be a working wife and mother, Shirley Conran asserts: 'It is important that you shouldn't feel guilty about working – and this is impossible. You have been conditioned to feel guilty. Accept it. Children instinctively know that your guilt about your work is your Achilles' heel and will use it when they are bored, or cross, to have a crack at you.' Both the women and the men we interviewed raised the issue of the guilt they sometimes felt about being a working parent. Indeed, Austin Mitchell still carried this burden even though his children had grown up:

'My kids are fine and they've turned out very well, although I've always had a terrible feeling that they wouldn't and that I would be scarred with that. One of the kids actually lives with us now, but yes, I think there is still a feeling of guilt. I think that I am a fairly irresponsible person who does too much and attempts too much, but I only feel that in moments when I'm down, I don't feel it most of the time.'

For Judy Finnigan, her guilt is most intense when it involves leaving a sick child:

'I feel awful and guilty, and often very tense because when they're ill, that means, that's the time they cry when you leave. I mean, most of the time they're quite happy, they're sitting having their breakfast and Claire's there who looks after them and it's all "bye" and a little kiss. But when they're ill, they want you and you have to put on a performance even though you leave feeling like a coiled spring. It's another major stress point for us.'

Linda Kelsey believes that feelings of guilt are, on the whole, pointless and self-destructive:

'I was talking to somebody else the other day who is also a new mum and I said, "I want to scrub the guilt off my list." I know that's easier said than done, but I do believe guilt is self-indulgent and if you are going to come to work and feel guilty, you're not going to do your job properly. You're not at home looking after the baby, so what the hell's the point of it. If I felt really guilty about not being with Thomas, I would have to stop working and find another sort of way of surviving.'

Victims of Spill-over

With the odd exception, almost all our stress survivors had experienced spill-over effects between the home and work/ social environment, which were usually negative in nature. This of course substantiates other recent research on successful people and executives, and is hardly surprising when one considers the high levels of emotional commitment often required from their jobs.

Undoubtedly, the pressures inherent in the divided loyalties experienced by many of our stress survivors were often similar regardless of whether they were male or female, and the importance of a supportive partner was emphasized time and time again. However, nearly everyone we interviewed maintained they were making positive moves to separate and better balance their work/home conflicts. This change in men in acknowledging the importance of the home/work balance was also emphasized by Joanna Foster:

'When we started the Pepperell Unit, we ran a series of workshops which we called Divided Loyalties. It ran on a Saturday in association with the *Guardian*'s Women's Page for working mothers. We then ran it in the week as well. At the last one, it was 50 per cent men and 50 per cent women and that was a sign of great encouragement to me. It's not only an issue for women any more. This was an indication of companies saying "The workforce is changing, needs are changing, we'd better put family issues on the agenda *now*."'

This was further exemplified by the recent study of British managers carried out by Richard Scase and Robert Goffee; indeed, it formed the thesis of their book *Reluctant Managers*:

As far as men are concerned, there appears to have been a shift in their personal priorities over recent decades. Our data would seem to confirm that men's unfulfilled career expectations, their increasing frustrations associated with programmes of organizational restructuring and the continuous redesign of their jobs are leading them to withdraw psychologically from work and to seek greater personal rewards in their private lives.

6
Work Stress

In the last couple of chapters we looked at two of the major aspects of environmental stress, namely stress faced at different stages of life and stress in the family. In this chapter, we will examine work stress and it is useful to note that, regardless of how one job may compare to another in terms of stress, in any job there are a wide variety of potential stressors. Researchers have identified five major categories of work stress which include factors intrinsic to the job, role in the organization, relationships at work, career development and organizational structure and climate.

Sources of stress

| Intrinsic to the job |
| Role in the organization |
| Relationships at work |
| Career development |
| Organizational structure and climate |
| Home–work interface |

INDIVIDUAL

Symptoms of stress

Individual symptoms
• Raised blood pressure
• Depressed mood
• Excessive drinking
• Irritability
• Chest pains

Organizational symptoms
• High absenteeism
• High labour turnover
• Industrial relations difficulties
• Poor quality control

Disease

CORONARY HEART DISEASE

MENTAL ILLNESS

PROLONGED STRIKES

FREQUENT AND SEVERE ACCIDENTS

APATHY

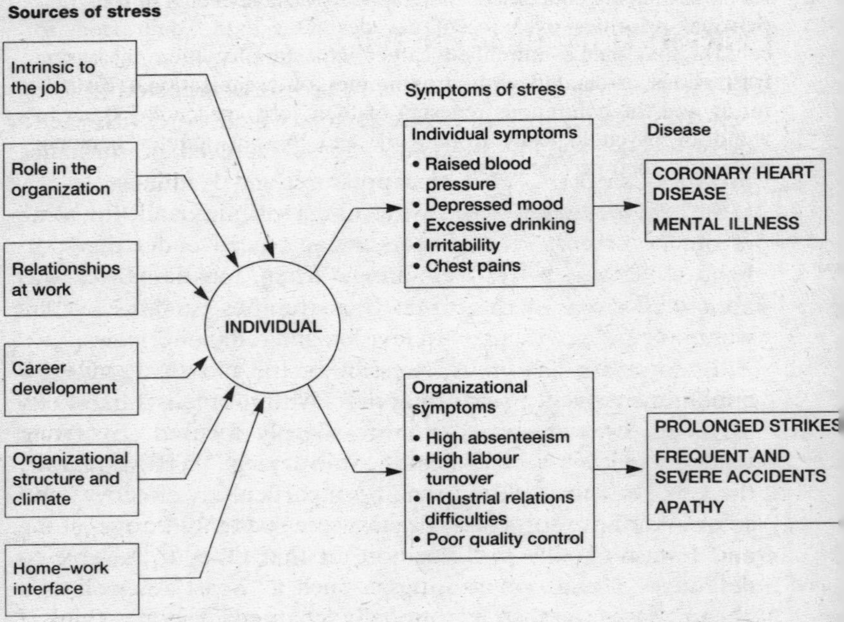

Figure 3: Dynamics of Work Stress

Common to all jobs, these factors vary in the degree to which they are found to be causally linked to stress in each job. When we questioned our interviewees about stress at work, not surprisingly, because they had all reached the top of their respective professions, career development issues were rarely mentioned. In addition, because of their power and status positions, frustrations linked to organizational structure and climate were not included on their agendas of work stress. In comparison, organizational workers lower down the status hierarchy sometimes complain they lack adequate opportunities to participate, complain they do not have a sense of belonging, feel they are not included in office communications and consultations and that their behaviour is unduly restricted. Nevertheless, our interviewees did mention a number of work stressors intrinsic to their specific job, issues related to their role in the organization and examples of relationship problems.

Factors Intrinsic to the Job

By far the largest category of work pressures reported to us by our stress survivors were those factors which were intrinsic to their specific job. In particular, these involved performance pressures, work overload, time pressures and deadlines.

Success inevitably brings with it high visibility and, for some of our non-media professionals, being placed under the spotlight sometimes proved daunting. When Joanna Foster was appointed Chair of the Equal Opportunities Commission she was bombarded with press, television and radio interviews:

'It got more and more stressful as the month of my new appointment grew closer. Interviews with journalists like Polly Toynbee, or whoever, got more sharply focused. Everyone tended to get my back against the wall saying, "Well you know, the EOC has no teeth, it hasn't been particularly effective" and so on. All those sorts of criticisms were suddenly thrown at me and I wasn't really in a position, at that time, to be able to defend it. Equal opportunities is such a "heart" as well as a "head" issue and so emotionally charged. I don't think I realized just how very public the job was and that has been very stressful. But, equally, it has also been mixed with the real excitement of suddenly having the platform to talk about the issues that I really believe are the really important ones.

'So, getting this job has been mixed with the pluses and the minuses. It does get the adrenalin going in a way that I think is absolutely wonderful now. Even if it includes appearances on *Wogan*, I know that if I want to mainstream the equal opportunities issues, then that's the price I'm going to have to pay – doing these terrifying things for the first time. And, there are lots of people out there saying, "Well, maybe equal opportunities is about me. It's about the way I live in my family, about child-care and elderly parents. And it's about me as a man as much as my wife." That's what I passionately want to do in the time I'm in this job, it's to get people whether male or female saying, "It's about me."'

Public speaking of any nature still terrifies Linda Kelsey and although she finds careful preparation helps to keep this fear in check, it can still lead to sleepless nights:

'I get absolutely terrified if I have to do public speaking of any sort whatsoever, even if I have to make an address at somebody's small leaving party in the office. For that thirty seconds before I knock on the table a couple of times and say so-and-so's going, let's wish her well and drink a toast, I sort of seize up inside.

'It's probably the one thing that gives me sleepless nights. It's got better over the years, but it's still ghastly for me. I no longer have the shakes hours before, but I still get them. I always rehearse, if I have to say anything publicly. Not only would I have written it down, but I would then learn it and have it in note form. I go through absolutely every possible angle, giving myself every back-up, so that I don't actually seize up, because it would be very easy for me to do just that. For me, that would be the worst moment. I did it on the radio the other week. I was being interviewed on *Woman's Hour*. We were talking about some survey that *Cosmopolitan* had done, it was all going quite fine, I'm always aware that I might be sounding very inarticulate but it was going all right. Then suddenly, I was asked a question to which I knew the answer quite well and I just said "eh" and nothing came out and it kept not coming out. I don't know how long this went on for but it was live radio and it seemed an eternity. Eventually, I managed to say something!'

Live performances and broadcasts were also seen as stressful by some of our personalities who were in the media, although most, such as Jonathan Dimbleby, thrived on the pressure:

'I do three live programmes a week. One on the radio on a Friday night, which is *Any Questions?*, then there's a live *Any Answers?* which is a phone-in programme on a Saturday. Then there's the live Sunday programme which is *One O'Clock*, plus all the other things I do as well. The demands and stress of a live programme are obvious, particularly if you are doing a big political interview in the middle of the week. It does get less stressful as time goes on though.'

Pamela Armstrong also adheres to the stress assimilation process which most 'performers' experience when they first start broadcasting:

'Stress is about being in situations that are extremely demanding. For instance, when I went to ITN and I had to learn to be a newscaster, it was demanding because I had never read an auto-cue before, so I had to learn how to do that. After an initial period of learning a new skill, the job became easier and more simple, but there was a necessary learning curve to go through.

'The same thing happened when I went to work at Capital Radio. That was the first time I did any broadcasting in front of a microphone. If you are in a public arena you do have to learn quickly, that can be stressful. Luckily, I had a patient and generous boss.'

However, due mainly to inadequate preparation, Stuart Hall recalled that a couple of his early live television experiences were nothing short of disastrous:

'When I first joined the BBC, I started in radio. I didn't find it stressful because I really enjoyed it. I think if you really enjoy doing something, you don't feel any stress. I did three months on radio, and television came along and they said, "You are possibly the brightest prospect we have ever seen. You are simply wonderful. You are going to be Number One on television." And like a fool, I believed them.

'So, I didn't study any television studio techniques and simply entered it. I swaggered in and thought I was going to be the bees' knees. I got away with it for a few weeks, then of course I fell flat on my face. Totally flat upon my face. I made a broadcast in my own style and didn't bother understanding the floor manager's instructions, so I ignored his instructions. I was so intent on my broadcasting, I went straight to the other end, collided with the weather forecast and made a balls-up of it.

'That was in London and it was a *big* one. I got on the plane at Heathrow, it stopped for half an hour in Manchester and then carried on to New York. I thought, "I am so depressed, I'll stay on the plane and go straight through to New York." My television career was at an end, it was finished before it even started. I knew I was finished.

'Anyway, I didn't go to New York – maybe I should have! So, a few weeks later the BBC rang me and said, "Look, you are a guy with talent, you blew that one, but we'll give you another chance." I had done some motorcycling commentaries for Castrol and Shell. I had written the commentaries and narrated them, they were very funny and had won awards for script-writing and narration. They said I was brilliant and I thought, well, maybe I am. They said, "Look, we have a motorcycle scramble in the Cotswolds – will you do it?" Now, the danger signs should have been flashing for me because I had never done a live motorcycling event. But, I thought, I'll go down the day before, get to know their riding styles, get to know the riders and I'll be OK on the day.

'So, everything went fine. I knew the chaps, I knew what I was doing – I was quite prepared and had done what I thought was the homework. Now, it snowed overnight. We went up to the Cotswolds on the Sunday morning for practice. I was still all right, but then came the thaw. The snow melted, it became mud, and every rider was obscured, caked in thick mud. Oh my God, I can't see the numbers and I don't know the guys covered in mud! It could have been anything riding round, it could have been the Ku Klux Klan for all I knew. I had that sinking feeling you get when you can feel all your innards and your brain dropping to your guts. All the flamboyance, wit, style, exuber-ant verbosity, the pure gold of the extrovert, turns to water and dross. What emerges is nonsense. The stench of failure filled the commentary box. My brain was numb. There was an emptiness, a loneliness, a greyness that flooded my desolated body, another bleak failure. What emerges is nonsense. All I wanted to do was escape – it was live TV. And, I don't even know to this day who finished first, second or third – I have no idea. Nobody else did.

'It was then it dawned on me that working in television meant total, dedicated professionalism. If I was going to master it, were I ever lucky enough to be offered a job again, then I would have to be totally prepared for it. There was no such thing as the glorious amateur going in, waving the spear.'

Roger McGough maintained that learning to cope with the stress of giving stage readings of his poetry actually helped to improve his performance, although some situations turned out to be more stressful than others.

'It's a funny thing to do the readings because you give yourself stressful situations all the time, which you cope with. The result of which is that you do better. It does however depend on the situation. Like a very rare one the other week, a place where it was the wrong situation – full of people who were there for Boy George and Gary Glitter. You want to get on and get off. But that's all right as really it's quite funny, although at the time it's stressful.

'But usually, you give yourself a situation that you can cope with. I go to Australia a lot for instance. Part of me thinks, why don't you just stay at home? You're giving yourself these big adventures – and I'm not really adventurous! I take the family over and it's difficult but I do it because the alternative is just to curl up in bed all the time!'

In contrast, today, Stuart Hall is a highly experienced broadcaster who not only enjoys his regular live television programme, but actually relishes the thought of something going wrong:

'I hope tonight that when I go on in an hour's time everything breaks down, as it did one evening after six months of present-ing the programme. People we were supposed to be interview-ing didn't turn up at the studio, the film broke down, everything fell apart. I looked at the floor manager in front of me. He was smartly attired in the most beautiful Fair Isle sweater, his earphones on, with his scribbling pad and an armada of fountain pens to scribble his autobiography. I turned to him for instruction, with ten minutes of the programme still to go. He reddened, coloured right up, turned his back on me, and shrugged his shoulders, as much as to say, "Well, you've got ten minutes of programme time, Charlie, now you fill it!"

'So when I started to talk about things that interested me and conversed about everything under the sun, I couldn't stop talking. Not declaiming, but *talking*. Communicating with people and conversing about everyday events, things in life I knew they'd be interested in. I imagined real people out there in the void. Afterwards, the team came on set. Sweat was rolling off everyone, and I was melting as well . . . I thought, "That's it, we've done it." That was the big test, ten minutes talking to millions of people and I enjoyed it! I was exhilarated!'

Performance pressure of another kind concerned having to sustain the same quality of work, particularly when our successful personalities had a reputation to keep up. At the time of our interview the Emanuels' new ready-to-wear collections were under public and press scrutiny for only thirty minutes, twice a year. 'I suppose our whole name is on the line,' said David. 'We've just shown Autumn/Winter and now we'll be showing in October, Spring/Summer. One's whole reputation is going to be channelled into this one day, not only into this one day but this one event that takes thirty minutes. It's difficult to show yourself even if you'd been given an hour and a half, never mind a few minutes.'

Being continually assessed like this was also highlighted by Helen Fraser as being a common pressure in the world of publishing: 'Publishing is full of little failures because in everything you do, you take a risk. It's very difficult, especially if you're an editor in publishing as it's a profession where you're constantly being judged. You're never any better than your last year. It's a bit like films, your bankability depends entirely on your recent successes or failures.'

The actual relative importance and monetary value of certain writing contracts could also initially increase stress levels for Roger McGough:

'When you take on a seriously done play like *A Matter of*

Chance, you knew it had to be delivered at a certain time. Then the next project I did was the screenplay for *Peter Rabbit*, proper money, a proper job. Suddenly, I start to think, can I do this all right? If they're paying me this much, they must be expecting a lot. But, once you start doing it, the pressure eases and you enjoy it. *The Wind in the Willows* was another similar sort of thing, a Broadway musical. It wasn't one of the great successes of all time, but it was quite interesting to do.'

While none of our stress survivors reported problems concerned with work underload or not being sufficiently challenged by work, work overload pressures were common. Two different types of work overload have been described by researchers. First, 'quantitative' overload refers simply to having too much work to do. On the other hand, 'qualitative' overload refers to work that is too difficult for the individual. In the first case, too much work often leads to working long hours, with attendant problems such as stress-related illness and increased cigarette smoking.

Jonathan Dimbleby gave the following apt analogy of work overload pressure:

'It's like watching those shots of Aintree you sometimes get at the Grand National when you see the horses coming towards you. You see all the fences very close together because they've been condensed in the lens of a camera. The stress is when you begin to feel that there are an awful lot of fences very close together in front of you and maybe you haven't quite got enough time to jump them all. Therefore, you're going to fall at one of them.

'There are occasions when I've misjudged what I can do, when I've just got to the edge of doing too much and I sense it. I then have to take a break, I have to make sure that I don't get into a suppressed panic. Now, I'm quite good at not getting into a panic because that's what you have to learn to do, doing my kind of job.'

Sir Terence Conran asserts that learning to delegate is a vital managerial skill which can help relieve work overload pressures:

'I remember when I was young, I hadn't learnt to delegate and things did get on top of me. I suddenly learnt how to get through life, achieve things and do things that I enjoyed, by building up a team of people around me that I was prepared to trust and delegate to. I think that is all part of the problem, people don't or can't believe that anybody can do anything for themselves – that, undoubtedly, is a cause of stress.'

Television controller Jonathan Powell agrees, but also points out a common frustration linked to high-flying executives:

'I'm now involved with programmes although I'm not actually making them, which is what I started out to do. I think that does add a lot of incredible frustration and it does build up your stress. You have to deal with the problem of giving the responsibility away and letting other people do things you might not have done. I find that pretty frustrating.'

Indeed, it was largely due to lack of staff support and subsequently an inability to delegate work which resulted in overload problems for the MPs Nicholas and Ann Winterton.

'I encourage schools and other groups from the constituency to come round the House, but you can only show them round in the morning,' commented Nicholas. 'In the afternoon, of course, not only is the House sitting but there are committees sitting – select committees, standing committees, all-party groups and some even sit in the morning. Therefore, you're committed to the House all day, so you work under great pressure. It's one of the great problems of the place and I'm not sure how you strike the appropriate balance.

'We're really very badly served. I do have a full-time secretary who actually comes up to the House now. However, I get approximately 300 letters a week and to deal with those as well as my responsibilities in the House, all the engagements I'm asked to do, speaking and receptions, luncheons and other things I'm involved with as a Member of Parliament, puts you under immense pressure. I personally believe that as a Member of Parliament, if you can justify the employment of a member of staff, you should be able to have that person paid for out of government or Parliament funds. I mean, Ann has got a substantial constituency of 66,000 and I'm even bigger with 77,000. In addition to everything else, I'm on the chairman's panel and I'm also the longest serving member of the select committee.'

'The lack of back-up is certainly a stress,' continued Ann. 'Take for instance a simple thing like being scheduled to go to a business lunch. It might be the Paper Federation or the Society of Motor Manufacturers and Traders. Now, their lunch might be at the Hilton or at the Dorchester. Not only do you have to do a full morning's work but then you have to try and find a taxi to get you there. You have nobody to do that for you, you actually have to go and wait for a taxi, or go on the tube, or get on the bus. And, you know that if it's pouring with rain, everybody's in a taxi, they're usually all booked and very few and far between.

'So, you have this pressure of trying to get there on time as well as having to arrange transport back afterwards. It's not as if, like ministers, mayors or chairmen of councils, you have cars to pick you up. I'm not saying that we want to get into quite that luxurious situation, what I am saying is there's a lot of allied, irksome, earthy stress involved with doing the job because you have to do everything yourself.'

Work overload pressures are commonly linked to time pressures and deadlines. In fact, Type A personalities are notorious for setting themselves impossible deadlines and feeling under constant time pressures. They also tend to underestimate the time available. Ask a random group of individuals to close their eyes and, without counting, open them when they think three minutes have gone by. The majority of Type As will have opened their eyes well within the set time period, whereas most of the Type B individuals will overestimate the passing of three minutes – or even fall asleep! In addition, recent research has shown that one of the other major pressure points for Type As is when they feel they have no control.

Like many of our stress survivors, Derek Jameson is a typical Type A whose life contains a continual stream of work engagements, time pressures and deadlines:

'Of course, I'm under immense stress all the time – I have been all my life and it's second nature to me. I've now gone thirteen weeks without a day off and the stress and tension are acute. It's never been worse than the current time. I'm writing a book and have a deadline of 85,000 words to produce in three months. I also have to run a daily radio programme, make two television series and do various other gigs like after-dinner speeches and opening bingo halls and so on.'

In the former Emanuel partnership, Elizabeth appeared to be more Type A than David and although they both enjoyed a certain amount of stress, the workload and continual deadlines could be problematic. According to Elizabeth Emanuel:

'You learn to recognize stress in the business and today is a very good example. You suddenly have a lot of appointments that you have to devote your entire attention to each one and you know that they're going to overlap. So, you start to get nervous and twitchy. However, it's one of the things that keeps us going as it happens so frequently and I find that unless you have some kind of stress in your life, I find I can't function properly.'

David Emanuel added: 'You are constantly faced with dead-lines from clients and it's no good saying the day before the ball, "I haven't quite finished the frock." You're faced with dead-lines for buying fabric because if you don't get your orders in, you won't get it delivered in time. There are deadlines for delivering and deadlines for showing. We did a show in March and we have to deliver to the stores by August, September time, particularly with the American stores. It's better if you actually have a deadline date as we can work to a timetable because that's how we've been trained. It's when there's a "looseness" in between seasons which I hate, but then there are other projects to do such as theatre or ballet projects. So, the first thing we always ask the client when they come here is, when is it for?, because even if we desperately want to do it, if the workroom is booked, then we can't fit that person in.

'Elizabeth will sometimes put impossible deadlines on some things while I try to be realistic. Invariably, however, she is right, which can be very annoying! She tends to say, "Look, we must do it, it could be this, this and this" and generally it works out great. It means of course working until two and three in the morning sometimes. Nobody can function like that. You can do it for a one-off project now and again, but obviously, you can't do it all the time, the body just can't cope.'

The most stressful situations for Elizabeth Emanuel involved those in which she felt she had no control, particularly when working under time pressures:

'The stress still comes if you are not given complete control – fabrics that you ordered may not arrive, the sampling may not be in the right colour and so on. The fashion show is the most stressful time, the guys who come to do the music haven't turned up and you know you have got to get things done by eight-thirty the next morning. What do you do? We've been in situations where you kind of black out almost, because it's so stressful. I think that's the way the body kind of protects itself, you just cut off. Around the time of the royal wedding, we had so much to do, that we just thought, "God – how are we going to do this? Help!"'

The introduction of new technology into the work environment has required workers continually to adapt to new equipment, systems and ways of working. In our book *Women and Information Technology*, frustrations associated with lack of control, particularly when computers broke down or mistakes were made by operators, were commonly-reported stressors. One of our stress survivors, Bel Mooney, described similar anxieties when her computer let her down at a crucial time while trying to meet a copy deadline: 'I haven't got a back-up disk so I'm really stuck. This happened to me last week. I've been ill for the past two days and I'm sure it was a direct result of that.'

'That's for certain,' interrupted her husband, Jonathan Dimbleby. 'She went to the doctor yesterday who told her her illness was due to exactly that and he's told her to adjust her life accordingly.'

Role in the Organization

Three critical factors – role ambiguity, role conflict and the degree of responsibility for others – are viewed as being major sources of role stress at work. Nevertheless, when an individual's role in an organization is clearly defined and understood and when expectations placed upon the person are also clear and non-conflicting, stress can often be kept to a minimum. Indeed, many of our personalities believed that the elevated hierarchical role in their respective professions had brought with it power and freedom of choice. Moreover, this bonus of control over work issues was seen by many as an important stress-reduction facility. For example, Jonathan Powell commented: 'I think the whole equation changes when you get to the top of something. You're in charge, there's no one above you to put pressure on you, so you're not working against anything. It's also to do with wanting control!'

Success for Roger McGough has also brought with it more control over the type of work he chooses to do:

'There was a tendency in the past to do too many things I didn't want to do. I found myself going round schools which is quite heavy work. It's good in that it's pioneering and the children like it, but I stopped enjoying it. It became a stressful situation, going to a different school every day and doing poetry readings. Often, you'd be given the sixth form in the morning and you'd think, it's really great this, and then they'd give you the third form, 3Z in the afternoon. You'd follow the noise down the corridor and the sound of the "bovver boots" and you'd have to go in and sort them out. I just felt like a performing seal, so I've stopped doing that now. I think what's important is that I write the stuff.'

Eddie Shah emphasized that being his own boss and having total control was an essential ingredient in his success:

'You see, I'm not a corporate animal, I'm top of my business and nobody can take me away or kick me out, because I've got nearly all the shares. Tom and I own all the shares between us. We are a perfect partnership. We row like hell and all the rest of it, but we have a perfect trust of each other, so we just do what we want.

'I want control of what I do with my life. It's about not having to report for duty or having to do this or that. So, we're not in a corporate environment and one of the reasons why I don't want to go public is then suddenly I would have a liability. I actually achieve a hell of a lot as I am at the moment.'

Ironically, Sir Terence Conran was about to relinquish this type of high status role at the time we interviewed him and described how this had affected him.

'I'm in a sort of peculiar position at the moment as, having been for most of my life both chairman and chief executive in my company, I intend to retire shortly from the Storehouse part of it at the age of sixty.

'About a year or so ago, I appointed a chief executive who has now taken on quite a major part of what used to be my role. Moving out from a position of being "The Boss" in every single sort of way, in that everyone came to see me, has been quite difficult. Whether it is called stress or not, I don't know, maybe you could call it that. Actually, having to step back and not take decisions that I've been used to taking and seeing decisions being made by somebody else; well, it's a difficult transition period. I suppose it's something everybody finds they have to do when they come towards the end of their career in business. By handing over to somebody else, I'm losing control. I know it will probably lengthen my life by doing it, and it's good for business. However, when you have had that sort of terrific pressure whereby every sort of major decision has had to be your decision, in the end; it's quite difficult to hand that on to somebody else.'

Surprisingly few of our interviewees admitted to the pressures of isolation on reaching the top. An exception, however, was Joanna Foster whose new job as head of a quango meant living away from home in Manchester a few days a week:

'Before I actually started this job, I got more and more anxious about it. About the uncertainty, and was it going to be right, and had I made the right decision? Am I going to be able to cope with it? What are my peers going to be like? And, above all, what's it going to be like being number one in an organization?

'That's been the biggest change, the change in role. It's got some wonderful pluses, but it's also got some enormous stresses to cope with, mostly to do with isolation. Who do you actually bounce ideas off, where do you get your feedback from and how do you keep in touch with what's really happening?'

Joanna's solution to these problems has been to initiate interactions herself as well as to join network groups:

'Last night I went and did what's called the Sylvia Pankhurst Memorial Lecture at Manchester Polytechnic and then went back with a lot of the group to the Pankhurst Centre. It was wonderful and I really enjoyed it. It has been very lonely up here in Manchester alone in my hotel room in the evenings. I don't actually know many people here and because I'm the boss, few may say things like, "Why don't you join us, we're going to the theatre tonight?" I think there's this built-in barrier of not daring to do that with the boss. And yet, it's exactly trying to build some bridges and getting to know people and Manchester which is very important to me and I'm going to have to initiate things in that direction.

'That's why last night at the Pankhurst Centre was really wonderful being with a group of about ten women. I really came back feeling, at last I've really got into some of the fabric of what's going on in this very enthusiastic and committed group. I really must get myself into some network groups here, otherwise I'm just going to freeze. And, I am most concerned about not losing touch with what the real issues are.'

Relationships at Work

Finally, other people – and our different encounters with them – can be major sources of stress. In particular, in the work environment, dealing with bosses, peers, subordinates and clients can dramatically affect the way we feel at the end of the day. Stress researcher Hans Selye proposed that learning to live with other people is one of the most stressful aspects of life: 'Good relationships between members of a group are a key factor in individual and organizational health.' In his book *Something Happened*, Joseph Heller once again comically illustrates this concern about work relationships: 'In my department, there are six people who are afraid of me and one small secretary who is afraid of all of us. I have one other person working for me who is not afraid of anyone, not even me and I would fire him quickly, but I'm afraid of him.'

The University of Michigan researchers defined poor relationships at work as 'those which include low trust, low supportiveness and low interest in listening and trying to deal with problems that confront the organizational member'. We discovered that a common behavioural trait in our stress survivors was that they tended to adopt a directive approach to relationship problems. In Sir Terence Conran's case, he sometimes resorted to bogus bouts of temper:

'Actually, the thing that perhaps causes the most stress is when you have to work with people that you don't get on with. You feel, what on earth am I wasting my time on trying to persuade you about this, because I know that you'll never understand and you're being obstructive. There's nothing like a good bit of fake temper to stir things up. I can just "put it on" and cause people to get their adrenalin flowing and get them excited about something.'

While Linda Kelsey admitted to not enjoying conflict situations, she was adamant about confronting such situations and dealing with them, even if it means having to sack someone:

'I'm not happy dealing with conflict at work, but I will confront things. I don't avoid tackling those sorts of issues such as having to tell people that things aren't working, that they're doing something wrong or something I don't like. I keep very much on a controlled emotional level and maintain an inner calm.

'However, sacking someone is very, very difficult. It makes me very nervous but however painful it is for me, I know it's more painful for them. So, you just have to do it. I may not do it very well but there's no nice way of doing it, you just have to sit down and do it. It's horrible. Again, I'm not going to feel sorry for myself when it's the other person who's really going through it. Maybe they deserve it, maybe they can't help it, but either way, it's pretty humiliating and nasty for them.'

This sort of assertive behaviour was very common in our stress survivors and is particularly relevant, taking into account research which shows that the most successful managers are the most assertive and have the most highly developed desire for power. According to Alberti and Emmons in their book *Your Perfect Right*, the assertive person is 'open and flexible, genuinely concerned with the rights of others, yet at the same time able to establish very well his or her own rights'. Generally, there is a great deal of misunderstanding about assertion – there are fundamental differences between assertive, non-assertive and aggressive behaviour:

Assertive: You are acknowledging your own rights and those of others.

Non-assertive: You are denying your own rights.

Aggressive: You are denying the rights of others.

Being assertive, therefore, is not about being bossy, aggressive or selfish. There are two main skills involved in being assertive – verbal skills and non-verbal skills. When being assertive, a person generally establishes good eye-contact, stands or sits comfortably without fidgeting and talks in a strong, steady voice, neither shouting nor mumbling. Assertive talk includes 'I' statements such as 'I think', 'I feel', 'I want', co-operative words such as 'Let's' or 'We could' and empathetic statements of interest such as 'What do you think?', 'How do you feel?'

Finally, the unpredictability of client behaviour was something Elizabeth Emanuel found stressful. Luckily, this was part of the job which David Emanuel actually enjoyed and consequently they were able to allocate aspects of their business work to suit their individual preferences.

'The biggest stress factor in our work is dealing with clients. David tends to do it more than me because it's a very, very stressful situation when people have expectations of what they want while you know what it is you are actually capable of doing. For some people, nothing is ever good enough. You soon find out which they are. Fortunately, not a lot of our clients are like that and we're very lucky, but it does happen sometimes.

'There's always this thing that you don't quite know how a client is going to behave, which is one of the reasons that I tend to stay away from the private clients, because I find that kind of stress just too much to handle. I can cope with things that are stressful under my control and when I've actually instigated the stressfulness, but I can't handle it when somebody else puts you in a stressful situation. David, however, doesn't get flustered by that sort of thing, whereas I will. My kind of controlled stress comes from designing a collection, doing the best I can and then seeing the reaction of the press.'

The Major Work Pressures

Common stressors intrinsic to our stress survivors' respective jobs included performance pressures, work overload, time pressures and deadlines. Further, these were often enhanced by individuals adopting Type A modes of behaviour, and almost all our personalities contended that work stress was worse when they felt the situations were beyond their control. Typically, gaining control and power were common traits in our successful personalities, although, ironically, many acknowledged that reaching the top had meant having to relinquish a certain amount of 'hands-on' control and they had had to learn to delegate. Predictably, they were all highly ambitious and productive individuals who were concerned about the quantity and quality of their work output. Most acknowledged that the stress incurred by performance pressure – particularly live broadcasts, stage performances and public speaking – had decreased as their experience and skills had increased. In addition, an assertive approach to management was the style most likely used, particularly in potential conflict situations at work.

In all the different aspects of home and work stress we discussed with our stress survivors, positive learning from past mistakes was something they raised time and time again as being an important facet of their survival. This was highlighted once again by David Emanuel:

'It was quite frightening at the beginning setting the whole business up, but you learn quickly, you learn by your mistakes and there are things that you just wouldn't repeat. Things like the cheque not appearing or people saying that they don't like the dress and returning it, when you know they're already worn it the night before because you've seen their photograph in the society pages! You just have to learn from your mistakes.'

7

Coping

For each individual, there are a range of stressors in life and work that will put him or her under stress. Once a person experiences stress, he or she will adopt a series of behaviours in reaction to it; these we call 'coping strategies or responses'. In most cases, these reactions will deal directly with the stressful situations, producing solutions or behaviours or circumstances that alleviate the stressors. For example, typical stressful events and adaptive behaviours might include the following:

Stressor	Adaptive Behaviour
Overwork	Delegates some work
Worsening relationship with spouse	Works to identify source of problem and agrees ways to improve relationship
Job interfering with family life	Negotiates with boss more 'family time' (e.g., less travel, fewer long working hours)
Feels 'undervalued' at work	Confronts issue with boss and negotiates better circumstances

Each of these behaviours takes a source of stress and attempts to deal with the underlying cause. However, sometimes the response chosen is inappropriate or ineffective in dealing with the situation. Below is a set of coping strategies which are maladaptive in that they do not deal with the problem; they avoid the issue and probably aggravate it.

Stressor	Maladaptive Behaviour
Overwork	Accepts work overload with result that general performance deteriorates

Worsening relationship with spouse	Avoids spouse by working longer hours or engaging in more activities outside the home
Job interfering with family life	Makes promises to the family he/she can't fulfil
Feels 'undervalued' at work	Loses confidence and becomes convinced of own inadequacy

In all of the above situations, there is something the individual can do to transform maladaptive behaviours, which are harmful to the person and those around him or her, into adaptive behaviours. It is also possible, however, that what was 'stimulating pressure' at one point in time can turn into 'debilitating stress' when the individual feels unable to cope, becomes anxious about these feelings and begins to adopt inappropriate or defensive behaviours. The purpose of this chapter is to explore how our stress survivors seem to cope with extensive demands, pressures and traumatic experiences, since all of these people have shown an enormous capacity to survive in the longer term. Then, we would like to suggest ways in which people in general might deal with the ordinary stresses and experiences of life, focusing on relaxation, lifestyle change and cognitive reappraisal.

Dealing with Loss

Many of the stress survivors seem to have been strongly influenced by their parents, and the loss of one or both had a significant impact on them. Jonathan Dimbleby can certainly vividly remember the effect on him of his father's (Richard Dimbleby's) death:

'It was a massive sort of quasi "state" occasion, and all of that kept you so busy. We had to behave like a sort of Kennedy family, going down the aisle and holding yourself together, knowing you had to behave properly, and absolutely to repress any emotions. And in truth, I did. I think if you were looking at me from outside you would say, "Yes, he in the English way of doing things, is coping very well." My mother, who had been quite astonishingly composed, got quite ill afterwards, which is not uncommon, from the sheer strain. It was very, very stressful, and then she came through all that and flourished. The sort of coming to terms with it was gradual. I remember moments of enormous uncontrollable grief, which would build up and then come out under quite different circumstances, at the end of a row or at the end of a conflict which appeared to be about something else. And I then recognized what it really was, and then I was a lot easier about it.'

David Emanuel describes his mother's death in a similar fashion:

'One of the relatives said, "Oh, you're so lucky to have such a huge family," and they all turned up obviously. All my family live in and around the town where my parents were living. And in a way we sort of had each other as buffers against the pain. Then there was an opportunity, there was a week, an opportunity of talking, and I made a conscious effort to talk to everybody because I needed to. There was no emotion, like we all refused to believe it had happened. You could see it quite clearly, you know, it's real, even though it's only a matter of days that you know that our mother's not with us, our mother's not going to be there. "No, no, no, she's going to," I said, "she's actually going to pull through." Gradually, then, you begin to share, don't you, and to keep talking about it, as well. The other problem is that after people die, you get support and so on, but then people go on with their lives, whereas you are still going through often more "realistic grief". Just because the funeral is over, people think it's gone, but it isn't, how can it be? Or people don't mention it, which is almost, in some ways, as though it never happened.'

These memories of loss (particularly of parents) and feelings of insecurity were recalled vividly, and often with emotion, by many of the stress survivors. While psychologists usually see these adverse experiences as traumatic and literally 'wounding', Cary Cooper and Peter Hingley in their study *The Change Makers* contend that they are important in the growth of the person as well, in developing their coping resources for later life:

As the physical wound produces healthy scar tissue often stronger than normal to protect the damaged area, so the personality may protect itself by defending vulnerable aspects of the psyche in similar ways, by compensating through a number of defence mechanisms.

Certainly a number of our stress survivors reported feelings of 'strength through adversity'. These traumas seemed to have resulted in a successful testing out of their 'survival skills', a psychological tempering which led them to a greater inner strength, self-sufficiency and independence, which served them extremely well in their later careers. This is particularly highlighted in the moving account by Stuart Hall of the death of his three-year-old son, Nicholas.

'So my television career was terminated, we had lost our first child, and then it was black. For three years we devoted our lives to him, took him wherever for whatever he wanted, had him walking around. Then he would get a little blue, a little short of breath . . . That was empty, that was the void, that was the real void, because it didn't unite my wife and myself, it divided us. We each went our own separate "ways of sorrow". She was depressed, and I was just desolate, very difficult to describe, it's like having a hole in your guts. Perpetual hunger pangs. It's just dark. You always feel cold, and I think always feeling chilled. Lonely, isolated. That's the critical watershed, a priceless son taken away when you have devoted your whole life to cosseting him. And that was a very black year, everything seemed to be falling apart.

'Well, we did have a daughter by then, a daughter Francesca, she was partially ignored, we devoted everything to Nicholas, and she was born a year later. For two years we hardly realized we had a daughter. And then eventually we said, "We must get the marriage together. We'll start again." I got on my hands and knees, and prayed for another child. And then a boy child was born, Daniel, who was almost a replica of Nicholas. And we finally cemented the marriage together. With two healthy children, happiness returned. Eventually I motivated my career back on the rails. I got back into television again by the skin of my teeth, by which time I had clued myself up as to exactly which way I should be going, and how I should be doing it.

'Yes, grief is personal, there's no sharing grief. I found even to this day. A pal of mine sent his son away to public school and university. His son was always a little depressive, a loner. And last year, at the age of twenty-six, his son committed suicide. Now, I can't communicate with my old buddy. I have no words to console him, because I know how private is the intensity of grief. People try to be pleasant, to be helpful, to restore happiness. It's impossible, grief is so personal. And the grieving takes time to work out of the system. It was very difficult for me, because I had always been immensely fond of people, I am a gregarious man, I love people. But with Nicholas's death I avoided people, I retreated. Yes, I really retreated. I have always been a happy, extrovert guy, and it was difficult coping because I had never been an introvert, at all, ever. And even though born under Saturn, I have never been saturnine. I have always had a great joy, I like to make people happy, I like to get in and mix with people. I like smiles, I like happiness, I don't want to depress people. I'm a very positive person, I'm never negative. I couldn't put on the sour face, even though I was dying inside. I still wanted to make a quip and a joke, and to say, how are you, what's happening. I didn't want people to concentrate on my private grief, because it was a great black emptiness of my soul, nothing could fill it. Consolation had to come from within, in my own mind. And the same with Hazel, my wife, she felt the same. There's nothing you could say. You couldn't put your arm around your wife and say, oh well, come on, and this, that and the other. It was as if there was a bridge and we couldn't cross it. We prepared, quite by accident, our own coping strategy. We now analyse our problems, and distil from them positive answers to them.'

Lifestyle Changes

For many who have had significant loss-related or other severe pressure events, there is always a period of reflection and consolidation. For the stress survivors, this had been a time of self-analysis, lifestyle exploration and change. In many cases, this period was precipitated by some outside help, from a therapist or doctor or partner. For example, Helen Fraser, a senior publisher with Heinemann, was able to deal with a long-standing set of relationship problems with the help of a therapist.

'I suppose, what had struck me in my mid-twenties while I was having an increasingly successful professional life, was that my personal life was completely dark. I kept thinking why, why is it? Because from my time at Oxford and on, I had very long, very unhappy and unsuccessful relationships with men, which had lasted more or less until I met my husband, Grant. On reflection, I began to think, why is this person so beastly to me, it's so unfair. And you know I suddenly thought this is no accident, you know. I've been in this situation since I was sixteen, more or less. It must be something to do with me. It's not to do with "the man", it's not to do with the situation, it's to do with me. And that's really what sort of pushed me to seek help. I wanted to find out why, exactly, I behaved the way I did. And that was tremendously helpful, because I think that I was very lucky. I had an absolutely wonderful therapist, who we discovered subsequently has been a therapist to all sorts of well-known people, but we just stumbled on her by chance. The curious thing about therapy is that actually in some ways it works even better when you stop, because then there's a point of real growth. It's first of all a crutch, it's then a lesson, it's then a tool, but then when you stop (I found certainly between about thirty-two and thirty-five), my confidence increased enor-mously, and my feeling I really could cope with things. I could cope with failure, and I could understand clearly what had happened ten years before. So I think it was terribly helpful, and I am sure I couldn't have coped without that absolute bedrock which it gave me. I am now able to cope with the ups and downs of a highly pressured business life.'

When the pressures got too great for Jonathan Powell, Controller of BBC1 TV, he sought the support of a doctor, who helped him to re-evaluate his patterns of coping behaviour, particularly when to say 'no'.

'About two years ago I went to see a doctor, when I thought I couldn't cope and I went through it all with him. Since then I've tried to deal with it in a more positive fashion, and cope with the effects it has on me. I'm trying to learn how to separate myself off from things that I can't control, and how to stop it building up; it's quite difficult. Certainly, there was a point two years ago, when I felt really very shaky, and since then it's gradually got better, but I don't think I've really solved it all. I find it quite hard to cope with my workaholism. You have to make a real effort to pull yourself up and tell yourself, and draw the limits of where your influence is and where your trust in people is – to draw up different criteria for yourself in what you're going to do and how you're going to trust people and relate to them. It's easy to get wound up, when you can see things going wrong. You've got to be clear where you cut yourself off. I've had to slow down quite a lot. I expected to have to work a lot harder than when I was head of drama, and I expected the hours to be much longer, the input to be much greater, but I've had to back-pedal a lot and stop doing things.

'When I was directly running drama [for the BBC], producing, you could zoom along at your own pace, wind yourself up, set yourself off, and off you'd go rushing round the place. In this job, I had to make a conscious decision to do what there is to do and not invent things for myself. I gave up coming into the office at seven o'clock, because I was getting fantastically tired and there was nothing to do. In my former job, I was inventing things to do, rushing around. But when it's not there, it came as rather a surprise, it took me quite a lot of time to teach myself not to do it, and to feel it was not encumbent on me to behave like a "pressured executive". I had to make a decision simply not to do it. When I was in charge of a bit of drama, I used to come in every morning at seven o'clock with this pile of work to do. I was taking things on myself partly because of the situation, and it dawned on me that, apart from the things you obviously can't do, I couldn't deal with everything. Being part of a huge organization like this, it's management structure, it's not like running your own business, it's completely different because actually you don't generate business. That's not to say that you're lazy, it's simply that the limits of what you can do are quite circumscribed, and what is foolish is trying to work outside them and not get too frustrated at things that you simply can't change. So I make a point of that. In the evenings I still have a lot of work to do. I have to watch everything that's on BBC1. Also, professionally, I have BBC2 and the other channels to keep in touch with, so arguably you could say the job never stops and, indeed, it doesn't, but now it's passive involvement.'

For Nina Carter, model, rock star and wife of Rick Wakeman, traumatic changes and poor health forced her to reconsider, and grossly change, her lifestyle.

'Well, I was a model and I was lucky, I was a very successful model. I travelled all over the world and later on after ten or so years of being a model, I then got involved with the pop business and I formed a band called Blonde on Blonde which, to be perfectly honest with you, was not a great musical talent. We looked great, and it was our image that made us. Well, I was very silly, I was a very silly girl, I did all sorts of things within the sphere of being a jet-setter, if you like – and all night clubs and just generally being a very immature, trendy sort of person at the time. I got myself in a lot of trouble. I gave up eating for about six months and lived on Complan and milk, and eventually became very ill and ended up in hospital having a very serious operation. After this, I took a look at myself – I'd gone down to five and a half stone, which is absolutely ridiculous. I said, I'm going to die if I go back to the people that I've been surrounding myself with, who quite honestly hadn't changed their lifestyle and were still offering me the same superficial friendship as before. I thought the only way out was to move out of this lifestyle, so I did. I moved right out of London, I just cut the ties, even with my best friends, and started a new life. I bought a dog and lived in a little cottage, which no doubt Rick will tell you about – I thought it was great and I had a nice laid-back sort of life. I used to go to the pub and drink half a pint of Guinness and I didn't want anything to do with the pop world or the rock world, and then I met Rick. We were looking for the same things, a family life and security.'

Two busy MPs, Ann and Nicholas Winterton, have a great deal of difficulty saying 'no' and adjusting their lifestyle to suit the job. The demands of the job frequently intrude into their private life and make it difficult to refuse invitations or constituents, as Ann Winterton suggests:

'I have to just say to myself, is it worth me going or accepting this invitation? I ought to go, I would like to go, there is something I can get out of it, but I only have an hour to do it. And unfortunately, I have to ask, is it really worth the hassle? You have to say to yourself, no, I won't do it.'

Her husband sometimes feels that people don't appreciate the pressures on MPs, and expect they have the kind of infrastructure that captains of industry possess. 'I attended three functions the other night, and at the second function someone said to me "Oh, Mr Winterton, is your car waiting outside?" I said I didn't have a chauffeur-driven car. I actually have to drive here, park and drive away.' MPs are expected to work long hours, to be readily available, in effect, to lead lifestyles that are accommodating to others, and difficult if not impossible to change.

This is also the case with people at the 'coal face' of television, particularly if they are a 'working together married couple', like *This Morning* presenters, Judy Finnigan and Richard Madeley. Separating their lifestyles is very difficult indeed, as Richard contends:

'If you like, all parents in a sense have to put on some kind of performance for their children; I mean, you don't have a blazing row in front of the kids or whatever. There are conversations you can't have in front of the children, things you can't do with the children, so when we're at home, we're parents, and when we're at work, we're at work. Working together, we're presenters and colleagues, and we're very much "on show". When we get to work, and if there are any sort of personal things we need to discuss or we've had a row in the car coming over, there's no way you can siphon off that pressure, because there are producers, researchers, directors, colleagues, all coming in needing your input.'

Judy elaborates: 'We try and shove it out to the back of our minds, and it generally doesn't surface again until we leave. Sometimes, when it's a particularly pleasant programme to do or something nice happens, we just forget it.'

Richard continues to develop the theme: 'Yes, I agree, but if we have a bad one . . . If it's a good programme then you're drawn together, but, I mean, we don't have arguments all that often. On those occasions, if it's a good programme, one is soothed and comforted by that. If it's a tough programme or a difficult one, anger has to be directed against somebody. When you talk about stress in our lives, it's all interlinked, it's all very closely interwoven, everything locks on to everything else. So if we have a stressful morning with the kids at home before we leave, we are coming stressed to work – we live stress. Everything is a stress in a live programme, so you have a stressful day there, and then after this programme there are meetings to be attended. We go through the script for the next day and that's a stress point, because there are always things we want to change and discuss and argue about with the producers. And then we get in the car and we drive home, and on the way home, we start that sort of shift from presenters and colleagues hassling out the problems of the day, to thinking, now, so and so has been ill or we've got to pick up so and so from the dentist, and we hit the house and it's bang. And on it goes, we're giving the kids their tea. Work now stops!'

Richard finds it difficult, in the hubbub of life, to identify his coping strategies.

'I would say in terms of coping strategies, I don't think we have any. That sounds like a joke, but I think that's absolutely right. We have no time to sit back and reflect on what we should do. On the rare occasions when we do get away together, I mean, very rarely, when, for example, our nanny will have the kids for the weekend, we feel guilty. We hate not seeing them [kids] at the weekend, because that is the time to be with them. Occasionally, rarely, for sanity's sake, we spend two nights on our own, Friday night and Saturday night.'

But the pressure of being a 'working together married couple' in the public eye permeates their whole lives, as Judy illustrates:

'This business of getting up so early and having to be "all cylinders firing", and really alert in the morning. You're tired and you think to yourself, "I've got to get to bed early," or "What time is it, we should be in bed." And when we go out to eat, and only occasionally do we go out for a meal, we want to eat by seven o'clock. Because we keep such early hours, we're usually the only people in there. We eat basically as soon as the babies have gone to bed, that makes it six-thirty to seven.'

Richard felt that some action was necessary.

'I'd say apart from grabbing the odd weekend, what we need is more time off. Actually what we've succeeded in doing for our next series, we've negotiated more time off than they were originally prepared to let us have. We've basically arranged to have four working weeks off in the next run, and for three of those four weeks we will go away alone together for a week, and the nanny will look after the kids. We're going away to the Canaries in November, we're going to Luxor in Egypt in February. You spend a fortune on these things, but we're doing something other than work – and then we're going to take the kids too. Apart from those weeks, the occasional night out, and the occasional Saturday night out, I would say the only coping strategy Judy has is to get to bed very early. And mine is not go to bed early, if I go to bed early I will not sleep. In fact, I will give myself an insomnia problem, at least I tell myself that. I can't do it, so Judy goes to bed very early like half-eight, nine o'clock. I will sit downstairs, watch television, read a book or whatever, which I suppose is my "personal space". It's not at all satisfactory, however, particularly because when I do go to bed, and I try to get into bed before twelve (I need less sleep than Judy), I might wake her up, which is a major stress point.'

Cognitive Reappraisal

Not only are our stress survivors, in the main, able to assess their lifestyle weaknesses, and deal with them effectively in the long run, but also they seem very good at reappraising or perceiving their stressful events in a way that is 'constructive', which allows them to bounce back more quickly. They seem able to engage in what Karl Albrecht describes in his book on *Stress and the Manager* as 'quick recovery', that is, 'the ability to bounce back from upsetting or stressful experiences'. Learning to recover quickly takes little more than an awareness of how you actually do recover. As Albrecht describes it: 'Once you begin to think about your emotional responses, you can recognize the process of returning to emotional equilibrium after a provocation has passed.' Jonathan Dimbleby illustrates this 'bounce back' effect, and how one has explicitly to highlight the events in one's busy schedule to come to terms with them:

'When things go wrong, when other people can be tearing their hair out, the one thing you can never afford to do is to allow yourself to panic; if you do, you're done for. You have to apply "ice cubes to your brain", and I can do that. I taught myself that. If he's tearing his hair out and saying to me, "Jonathan, we're in trouble," I say, "Don't worry, it's all going to be all right, don't worry, I can handle that; just give me the cue, just give me the time, it's all right, I'll handle it all." And you feel very much in control, so long as you never allow that anxiety level to rise too high – it's a discipline. Some people, however, can't live without panic. There are producers who can't do it any other way. They only get their "kicks", if they do it that way (in a state of panic or at the knife-edge). You just say to yourself, "You have to deal with your nerves," because there is a flow of adrenalin. And you're thinking, God, this is a one-off thing, this interview that you're about to do or this programme. If you blow it, it's blown, you can't say, well, let's do that again. It's got to work, it has that dramatic quality, as well as that forensic aspect. But when the "fences" get too high and there are too many of them, I must back out of something. I must pull out, I must say "no" to something. When I feel that those fences are coming, even if they're quite big fences and quite close together, and I can ride them, then I have it under control, and I don't feel the stress. Unfortunately, I tend to think when I'm saying "yes" to something, that I'll be able to do it, and probably be able to fit it in somewhere down the road. I then get close to it, I get a sudden "I can't do it." Then, I cope with it best by making a note of what I've got to do, and all the things involved, so I can get it out of my brain and on to paper. By appraising the expected pressures, I can cope. If I take today, you came this morning, I've got a meeting when I get in [to the BBC]. On Sunday, we're doing a programme in Paris, which is extra complicated for all sorts of reasons. And on Friday, I've got to go up to Solihull for *Any Questions?*, and I've got to finish a lecture which I'm giving about the freedom of broadcasting from the radio. In addition, I'm still preparing (which we were working on yesterday) an interview with

Kinnock, which is a full hour long. Now there was a point last week when I looked at this week and thought, uh, uh, it's too much, and I then just sat down and thought, no, let's work it out. I've got two hours there, and I've got four hours there, I won't go out on Thursday evening, I can use Thursday evening to get the last part of this thing finished, and then you relax, and then you're OK. And then the real stress, you go and play tennis! The great thing about tennis is you can only think about the tennis, otherwise, you're useless.'

Jonathan's wife, the author Bel Mooney, also seems to be able to adopt the same helicopter view of life that enables her to cope.

'There's this book that has an aerial view of an executive with his 'phones, two 'phones and a kite on the cover, so it actually is very, very narrow casting. I found that very limited because stress at work, stress in life are not separate in any case. The executive who's under stress at work will take it home and that will affect his marriage. The point is everybody has troubles, I mean, life isn't perfect, and I think one of the first ways of coping with it, is to actually say, there will always be a shortfall of happiness, I can't achieve everything I want to do. And I think once you actually say that, and then decide to get on, you're there. There's a line from Ibsen I have written in my filofax, my executive filofax, at the beginning, and it says, "Think, work, act, don't sit here and brood amongst insoluble enigmas." And I look at it every day because in life that is all you can do, think, work and act.'

This phenomenon of 'quick recovery' would be very useful in business environments or the entertainment industry, or any job where people tend to find themselves drawn into personal confrontations where they are quite likely to experience anger and a full-blown stress response. In situations like this, as Dr Albrecht explains, 'our higher level mental processes will probably not be functioning very well. However, at a certain point, your emotions will begin to subside and you will realize that you are angry. That is, you will experience your anger as an intellectual concept as well as a physical feeling.' Dr Albrecht states that, at this point, you have the option to continue and aggravate your angry feelings by 'rehashing the provocation, rejustifying your position, reopening a new attack on your adversaries, and becoming newly outraged by their unreasonable behaviour'. A 'quick recovery' approach would suggest you stop this 'negative circular approach', become more rational and less conscious of your need to 'win'. This seems to be a characteristic our stress survivors display, time and time again. Victor Kiam relates an incident that demonstrates this:

'There's a lot of work and a lot of problems just now. We just had a major "brouhaha" last night. Ten years ago I would have called in everybody to the company and ate their butt out for what happened. But last night I just sat down, and thought about it, and said, "Well, I can't correct it now, what's the sense in calling everybody and beating everybody up." When I get back to the US, I'm gonna have a meeting and say, "Look, you made a mistake, try not to do it again."'

Social Support

Each individual meets the world daily with a complex set of physical and emotional characteristics, coping styles, values, a particular history of relationships and of coping effectively or ineffectively with life's stresses. Despite the importance of this individual make-up, it has been shown time and time again that many people need the positive and nurturing support of others, such as family, friends and colleagues. This support system can often act as a moderator of the effects of stress. Many of these 'supports' provide problem-solving, listening skills and acceptance that can relieve stress, even though they may not be able to solve the specific problem.

The family is particularly important as a social support unit. It provides its members with a history of how to cope; of how members lived, worked and dealt with problems of human existence. This was particularly well done by the extended family of years past, where each family member had a wider pool of experience available to help advise them about the world of work or life generally. The absence of the family support system, and its effect, can be seen in Derek Jameson's case.

'Life was a struggle on the streets. I still have dreams, nightmares about it. Every time I dream, I don't recollect them, I try to block them out and forget them – I refuse to remember them. But when I do wake up in the middle of the night in a cold sweat, which happens all the time, I can remember the dream, because it's been a few seconds earlier and it's always about my insecure childhood, always. It puzzles me that a person can be haunted, a successful, famous rich person in his late fifties, as I am now, by events of fifty years ago. I had to fight for my own independence, for attention. Yes, I've been doing it all my life. You have to learn to stand on your own two feet, you can't trust anyone, can't rely on anybody. You can't ever call on anybody's assistance, when you grow up like I did, you are a loner. You have to fight all your own battles, and those people you depend on most often let you down, and so there is a tendency, I think, to get the first blow in, to push them away before they reject you. This was a syndrome I was going through during my childhood, nobody to support me or to rely on, and it stayed with me the rest of my life.'

The significance of the loss of parental support can also be seen in Jonathan Dimbleby's dreams about his father, and the loss of this relationship to him.

'I dreamt a lot about my father for a long, long time. These were regular dreams, as well as frequent ones. I couldn't give you a clear picture of what they were about, but they always were of a character that made me wake up feeling a terrible sense of loss . . . I'd wake up in the morning thinking I just don't want to go through this day, and it would take at least an hour or two to begin to get myself back into going again. And I was surprised by that. These dreams continued for many years after his death. It doesn't happen now, although I can still get caught, and I know it's also true of the rest of the family.'

The importance of family and friends as support systems is best illustrated by Joanna Foster, the Chair of the Equal Opportunities Commission:

'Just being with my family, sitting down and eating with the family, is just a wonderful way of sharing and of loving. Laughing has always been a great stress relief in our family. I remember when we first went to the States, when we moved from France, that was a move I wasn't actually keen on, I was ready to come back to the UK. I was really quite depressed when we moved there, because I wasn't allowed to work and I really felt no control over my life at that point. We realized after about three months in the US, we hadn't laughed *with* anyone, because we didn't know anyone there. So we had actually to start the whole process of making friends, which we'd never had to do before. Because at INSEAD [the French Business School] there was a ready-made international community, and it wasn't until we actually met a couple with whom we did a great deal of laughing, that we realized how important laughing is with friends and having fun with friends. So friends have been very, very important. That way you can completely relax and be "you".'

Linda Kelsey also feels that friends and colleagues can provide the social support when under pressure which allows you to 'do your own thing'.

'I must have said this lots of times before, but the greatest good luck I've ever had, is working with really supportive women who've been my mentors, who spotted something in me, which maybe I haven't spotted in myself. So, instead of me being the "pushy one", which sometimes people have to be to get themselves noticed, I had people who were in effect doing that for me, supporting and helping me.'

Friends also allow you to express your feelings, to let your emotions out, as Linda Kelsey continues: 'I have always managed to sleep, but when I am under stress and have a close friend at hand I can cry a lot, which I think is quite good. I like to have a really good sob. I know I wouldn't want to do it in the middle of the office, for example, but it is good and healthy for me.'

As well as the family and friends providing social support, some of our stress survivors also rely on the church or religion. Roger McGough feels that his Catholicism is a bedrock, always there if he needs it.

'I suppose that religion provides me with social support. I'm a Catholic, so I go to church. It's a feeling that you're part of the community and saying prayers and things, makes me feel good. I didn't particularly turn to religion or Jesus during bad times, but it was always there. It is part of my background really, a sort of set of rules given to me as a child, which sometimes you reject. I even rejected it, because sometimes it becomes harder to follow. I just kept on with it though; it's always been important to me. I'm not a born-again Christian, I'm a cradle-Catholic.'

The influence of religion is also evident in Gloria Hunniford's life.

'I was never forced to go to church, but my pattern was I went to church and Sunday school five times on a Sunday. I went to children's service at ten o'clock, I went to main service at eleven, I went to Sunday school in the afternoon, I went to church in the evening and then I went to what was known as the Christian Workers' Union, which was really just like a kind of prayer meeting thing. To be blunt, there was nothing else to do on Sunday, everything was closed in Northern Ireland, social life revolved around the church. A lot of young people went to church and so that was it. So, when an American evangelist, from Billy Graham's organization, came along, I got caught up in all that and was "saved". I walked up to the front and was saved, it wasn't actually Billy Graham, I don't even know the name of the evangelist, but it was one of his brigade. I remember coming home and saying to my parents, "You know, I've been saved tonight and I'm *not* going to sing any more, I won't go to concerts any more." I believed that if you sang in public or if you went to parties or dances or anything like that, you'd go to hell. In a way, I was too young to understand what it was all about, I was thirteen or fourteen, but nevertheless, it felt good, I had to say it felt great, and so life began. I had to give my parents their due, they never said, are you sure this is the right thing, and I said to my dad, "I won't be singing at the concerts any more." I was sorry about that, but I felt it was something I had to do. All my friends were up front and "saved", and leading the so-called good life, and behind the scenes they were going to the pictures or going to dances. Then I thought this couldn't be right, it couldn't be all "hellfire and brimstone", that if you went to the pictures and dances and enjoyed yourself, you're going to go to hell. But religion has always been a support for me, from even those early days.'

Relaxation Techniques

Learning to relax is essential to our stress survivors, and many of them engage in a range of relaxation exercises or pursuits that achieve the same health objectives. It is obvious that the body needs time to relax and recuperate from the effects of everyday stress. Some people can dissipate stress, while others merely 'bury it' within themselves. This latter kind of stress reaction can reflect itself in a variety of personally damaging behaviours, such as excessive coffee or alcohol consumption, cigarette smoking, drug taking and so forth. Martin Shaffer in his book *Life After Stress* highlights some of these negative coping reactions:

Pausing Activities	Purposes	Effects
Smoking cigarettes, tobaccos	Pick-me-up, pausing, arousal, social activity	Increased energy, nutrient drain, poor sleep, indigestion
Drinking coffee or tea (non-herbal)	Pausing, arousal, social activity	Energy boost, nutrient drain, poor sleep, indigestion
Drinking hard alcoholic beverages	Pausing, social activities, central nervous system depressant	Energy drain, digestive imbalance, potential brain impairment
Eating sugary or highly refined foods	Pausing, arousal, pick-me-up, social activity	Poor nutrition, possible low blood sugar, possible indigestion

Fortunately, many of our stress survivors are people who avoid these negative coping strategies and engage in exercise or relaxation techniques or other strategies to reduce the pressure. Nicholas and Ann Winterton are regular members of the House of Commons gym; indeed, Nicholas was one of the founding members. They both feel that it is essential to use the facilities, although they realize that it is very difficult for many Members to do so, specifically government ministers. But they are disturbed by the fact that only roughly fifty out of 650 MPs use the gym facilities, particularly when they suggest that the number of MPs who have heart attacks is roughly twice the national average. Ann Winterton feels that exercise is important in keeping you on top of the job.

'Physical exercise is the most wonderful thing, like yesterday, we've had this terrible, terrible week. Yesterday was hell for me, and I thought I've got every good reason for not going to the gym, but I went. I actually missed just one exercise out, because I had an important appointment with the Prime Minister, and I turned up looking very flushed, but never mind. And I felt so much better for having been, you can cope so much better. So you've really got to "write it in" and say, no, I won't make these telephone calls, no, I won't sign my post, I'm going to do my exercises.'

And as her husband, Nicholas, reinforces: 'I've always said that although exercise is physically exhausting, it is mentally relaxing. It is the mental pressure that is the problem for MPs, not so much the physical.'

Jonathan Powell also feels that exercise is important, but as part of a larger life plan.

'I go down to the gym near where I live. Not as often as I should like, but at least a couple of times a week. I keep trying to go every day, but I don't seem to be able to make it. A couple of years ago I went to see a doctor about exercise. I was also advised on doing deep breathing exercises, which I find extremely helpful. Going to the gym is only part of my stress coping, along with doing deep breathing, leaving work early and not feeling guilty, and finally, I occasionally take a day off every month or two, so that I can do things I haven't had time to do, whatever that happens to be.'

Pamela Armstrong, on the other hand, engages in exercise as a means of extending her energy, the by-product being psychological relaxation and relief.

'I exercise a lot, but not for relaxation, I do it because it gives me more energy. One of its side-effects is relaxation. I do it to keep fit and it stops me getting ill – I rarely get colds or flu. I seem to have a robust constitution, which has stood me in good stead for the times in my life when there were periods of heavy workload. Exercise actually makes me physically stronger – one of the side-effects, happily, is that it is relaxing. Sometimes I walk, sometimes I swim, sometimes I don't do anything, sometimes I read a book. I don't have any one specific thing that I do every day religiously. I'll walk, for instance, if I'm in the middle of London and have a meeting. Though it's a luxury in terms of time, I might walk to it, from quite a long distance, and I'll take my sneakers with me because it's a very beautiful city, and it's delightful to look at the architecture.'

Many of the stress survivors have specific passions for exercise. For example, Jonathan Dimbleby plays tennis regularly and feels if he stopped he might have withdrawal symptoms.

'I mean, I'm lucky in that I can go to bed late and get up very early, and put in a longer day than most people can. Six hours' sleep is plenty for me. In fact, I have less than that, but I reckon six is nice. I mean this morning is not an unnatural morning. I got up at six, just before six-thirty and I went and played an hour's tennis at seven, which I do, and then came back and had breakfast. It's the best time to exercise, I love it. You know what it's like with jogging, with joggers, it's ludicrous. You become obsessed, become addicted to it. I am addicted to playing tennis, I play three times a week. It makes me feel good. Sometimes I feel if I don't do it for two or three days I will begin to feel withdrawal symptoms. I need the buzz, so I get up quite early generally.'

Rick Wakeman is obsessed by golf; it keeps his mind off other problems and is totally absorbing.

'You can't get rid of stress because it is always around you. Most of it is caused by financial problems that people have, it could be the children playing up, it could be anything. Most stress, I think, is not actually caused by the individual himself, but by the things that go on around him. I find that golf in this regard is very useful, because I still have a severe amount of stress and strain. For me, golf works tremendously well – it's been a fantastic stress reliever. For the past four years, I've been out at least once a week, I've gone out and played hard. You meet all sorts of people in different walks of life – for four hours I'm with myself or with other people. Any aggression I have, I can take out on that little white ball. The odds are I'm going to hit one great shot for the day, and it can set you up and relieve a lot of tension. I've seen friends arrive at the golf course – people especially in the entertainment industry – who have arrived in a terrible state, because something happened the night before – their agent dropped dead, etc. But, by the time they've finished their round of golf, they're perfectly relaxed people again. They are once again "human beings".'

Working out in a gym seems to be the typical activity of many of the stress survivors. Gyms are accessible in big cities and offer quick results, as Roger McGough describes:

'I go to the gym actually most days. I used to play five-a-side football a lot. I always used to play sport when I was at university, all the time, badminton, table-tennis, then when I went to live in Chelsea, I joined the gym there. So, I've always exercised or taken part in sport of one kind or another, and I've always enjoyed it. Doing something very static wouldn't do. I like to sweat, so I go jogging. But I like gym-work better than jogging, because if I have to jog too far, I get bored. I'd rather go and do aerobics or whatever, where you sweat quickly.'

Away Breaks

In addition to engaging in relaxation pursuits, almost all of the stress survivors feel that they either frequently or occasionally need 'R & R', a complete break from the pressures of a Type A lifestyle. Ann and Nicholas Winterton feel that unless they 'get out of the country' for a holiday, it is just about impossible for them to take a break. Ann highlights the problems:

'In a way, it [the job of an MP] can be a rod for your back, because you are never off duty, unless you actually leave the country. And this is the one thing we've learnt, and especially now I'm earning. We ensure that we actually go away on holiday much more often than we did before, because we feel it's necessary to totally unwind. Of course, our children come with us, on and off, depending on if they can. And we love it. The pressure of the job can build up in a stress bank. For example, if you go to a social function, you are being torn apart if you want to go on to something by say eleven o'clock, everybody knows you've got to go out, but they want more. As you're going out the door, everyone will be grabbing you to talk to you. You get somebody who will get you in a corner and you can't get away from it. You feel enormous conflict, you say to yourself, I've got to go, but I've got to be listening to him as well, I've got to make a note of what he's saying . . . this is real stress.'

Nicholas reinforces the constant and unremitting problems facing MPs, and the need for them to take holidays away from the pressures:

'The demands upon Members of Parliament are very much greater today than they used to be, and they're growing. Some of it is the responsibility of MPs themselves, because they have now become solicitors, they have become accountants, they have become social workers, they've become citizen advice bureaux experts, they are everything to everybody. And I mean, I had a call only this morning from a constituent with a housing problem. I have nothing to do with housing, but he said, "Mr Winterton, I can never get hold of my local councillors."'

Joanna Foster also emphasizes the importance of a break, of taking a family holiday: 'I believe in holidays passionately, that everyone needs to take them. It usually takes me a week really to unwind, and I nearly always feel very ill at the beginning of holidays, because when you stop running, you begin to feel terrible. But at least I recognize that, and now I can plan that we have three or four days at home before we go anywhere.'

Even the entrepreneur and supposedly workaholic captain of industry Victor Kiam feels that family holidays are an essential tonic and necessary social support function for the family: 'Every summer, Christmas and spring, my wife and I and the kids take vacations. In fact, my wife and I for fifteen or twenty years never took a holiday alone. Indeed, we even took our dog, Omar. We have always gone *en masse*, and to me it's just been a wonderful adventure. I enjoy every minute of it. The peace, the family, the togetherness.'

Eddie Shah felt the pressures from his personal and business crises accumulating and, by the end, he and the family were in desperate need of a break, so he took them away to Hawaii for six weeks, and didn't look back.

'I hadn't had a break with the family, we'd had Jennifer's illness, then the newspaper dispute which came fairly straight after that, then the *Today* fiasco, then we bought the Warrington Guardian Group, and we had to rationalize that. So, I've sort of had four or five years of fairly solid pressure. I then said, we're going away for six weeks, and we went to Hawaii. We spent six weeks totally away from everything. I had only one business telephone. I trust my managers, I trust them to run everything.'

But this trust does not extend to all our stress survivors; some of them feel reluctant to take holidays. Derek Jameson highlights this dilemma:

'In newspapers, it's a joke, for if the boss, the chairman, the proprietor tells you to take a holiday, you fear the worst. Maybe, when you get back to your desk, it won't be there! There is that kind of high-powered commercial politics about. So, I'm never very easy or comfortable or relaxed on holiday. I'm always worrying, I should be there doing the job. This is all kind of an instinctive response. Thinking about it logically, I've never wanted to work all my life. I'd rather sit in the sun reading the paper, I'm not a grafter by nature. I mean, some people from the minute they're born they've got to graft; if they're going to succeed the only way they can possibly do it is to work harder than anybody else around them, and that's been my situation. I envy those people who get the breaks without having to do much for it.'

Jonathan Powell felt in a very similar situation for a number of years:

'I was quite bad at taking holidays, though I do now. I spent a long time not taking holidays. I told myself I didn't think I needed them, because there was always something to do. But I guess it was because I didn't want to go away. Looking back, I was obsessed, because it meant so much to do well at work, I got very nervous about leaving. I think it probably was a concern about what might happen at work in my absence, although I didn't think so at the time. I just spent a lot of time not having holidays.'

There are also the odd individuals who need to take holidays by themselves. They need to get away from everything, to be on their own. Roger McGough is one of them.

'I don't talk generally about things I worry about. I tend to keep it to myself. There are some things, obviously, I talk to my wife about, but often I will just write poems instead: Here is one called "Worry":

> Where would we be without worry?
> It helps keep the brain occupied.
> *Doing* doesn't take your mind off things,
> I've tried.
>
> Worry is God's gift to the nervous.
> Best if kept bottled inside.
> I once knew a man who couldn't care less.
> He died.

*(Melting into the Foreground
1986, Viking Press)*

But I do like to get away on my own, usually courtesy of the British Council, or a writers' conference abroad. I do like to be on my own, it's exciting, being thrown on your own resources in a foreign country. Perceptions are heightened and I write continually. Beyond three weeks though I begin to get panicky and want to go home. I feel guilty and I get worried. So on long trips now I try and arrange for the family to come with me, as we did last year, to Australia. But I like being away and I like going on my own. I also enjoy working at home, being with the baby, Matthew, bathing him and that. But then I need to get away, and switch my mind off. It would be very tempting to spend the whole day with him, but then I wouldn't get any poems written, and so I ration the time and probably don't see much more of him than a father who's been out at work all day.'

There are others who can relax on holiday only when they are working; it seems to be part of the therapy and a way of keeping the work down when they return. Sir Terence Conran is one of them.

'I mean, even when I go on holiday, which isn't that frequently, I always work when I'm on holiday, and I enjoy it. I've got a house in France, and I'll go and sit out in the garden and set up a table and work there. My family moan about me always working – the other day one of my children said to my wife, "Hasn't he been a rotten father," but actually they rather admire you for it. Work is relaxing, but if I think that things are out of hand, I find it stressful. I loathe things being out of control, and things not being done in a timely way, I cope by working harder to catch up. One of the problems about going away on holiday is you come back and find a desk that high with papers. That is one of the most horrible experiences for me, to feel I have all that work to deal with and that I've got to get it cleared up. I am actually going on holiday on Thursday, and it will really upset me if I haven't cleared everything off my desk, but I'll be taking some of it with me. I've got a lot of things (work) to do on holiday that I'm looking forward to doing.'

Doing It My Way

Given the idiosyncratic nature of these successful stress survivors, it should not be surprising to find that most of them also have highly individualistic ways of coping with the everyday stresses and strains of life. These range from listening to the *Messiah* quietly by oneself, to having a weekly massage, to cooking. Derek Jameson's remedy to the pressure is a centuries-old technique, called Thermogene wadding:

'There's an old-fashioned remedy called Thermogene, it's a kind of thermal wadding. You sprinkle water on it and it brings out the heat, and I shove that on the back of my neck, where my stress comes out. Last night, when I went to bed, I shoved a great lump of this orange cotton wool on the back of my neck and I feel much better today. I suppose I psyche myself up to the belief that this Thermogene wadding, this old-fashioned remedy going back centuries, is doing me a lot of good. And, so it does.'

Elizabeth Emanuel finds that physical remedies are also helpful to her, particularly body massage:

'You just sit and try and clear your mind, it really does actually help, so I've found vitamins and massages very useful coping techniques. A dose of vitamins can really help. I have a massage every week, it doesn't really last that long, but I just find it's so important. If, for one week, I have to do without it, it really affects me. During the week, my muscles tighten up and I get very, very tense. When you have the massage, the whole thing just eases out all the muscles, and also I do breathing exercises as well – I find that such a relief. It's almost like a therapy, and it helps me to get through the week. David goes to the gym as well. I'm going to start going to the gym too, because the fitter you are the more able you are, and also because when your body produces the adrenalin, it's actually bad not to have anywhere for it to go.'

Linda Kelsey also uses deep tissue massage as a method of relaxation.

'I do some physical exercise, but I have a bad back so I started to go for a massage. That was lying on a table having deep tissue massage for an hour. It started because of my back, but I realized it was also making me feel much better, reducing the tension. The strain is sure to show up somewhere; mine shows up in my back, although sometimes it shows up in my stomach.'

For others, the best way to relieve stress is through their stomachs, by cooking. Sir Terence Conran finds solace in this pursuit.

'The other thing for me is that I enjoy my food very much indeed. I actually cook myself, it's the most pleasurable thing for me and is a form of relaxation. I go out and buy the food or go out into the garden and pick it, and then cook it, and sit down and eat it with friends. I find that eating dinner over a couple of hours or something like that is a very relaxing thing to do. I can never understand these people who grab a sandwich and who are not interested in that period of relaxation that a meal can bring. I try to do that most evenings. I am involved in the restaurant business, it's an area of professional interest as well, but it is something that I am passionately interested in, and it is, in fact, something that I should probably spend more time doing.'

So does Joanna Foster. She contends that the best way to switch off work is to cook: 'Cooking is something I always find marvellous, you know, just getting into it and just cooking.'

Bel Mooney likes the peace of great music and solitude: 'I do know that religious faith is a great consolation to people, even just lying down listening to the *Messiah* on a record, you know, as a sort of form of meditation on a higher level. I mean, in a way for me I would rather do that, that would be my way of coping, to lie on the floor and put the *Messiah* on.' On the other hand, religion for some can mean guilt and more stress, as Roger McGough highlights: 'I felt guilty when my mother was ill, dying. My sister was looking after her and I was away a lot. I wasn't there enough for my mother and I felt guilty about that. Then, of course, in my younger days I felt guilty about sex, and all that sort of thing. I do try to consciously live in a Christian sort of way, to be aware of other people, that sort of thing really . . . It's this Catholic thing, I always feel guilty whatever I'm doing.'

Others tend to cope by staying away from emotional situations, perhaps burying their feelings. Austin Mitchell reflects this type of reaction, which is quite common among some of our stress survivors:

'I didn't want to let constituents down, so I think I'm still programmed to duty in that kind of fashion. In career problems, I tend not to blame myself, just to say "hard luck" or blame other people, but I also sulk, although I don't get depressed. I'm not a depressed person, I sometimes wonder if I'm so shallow that I never get depressed. I just ignore things, I don't like unveiling emotions, I don't like emotional situations, I always try to shy away from them.'

As we have just seen among our stress survivors, they tend to use a wide variety of coping strategies to deal with the pressures and demands of life and work. We thought it might be useful to provide the reader with a questionnaire to help to identify some of these different types of coping styles. This scale is from the Occupational Stress Indicator, and is broken down into six different coping strategies: social support, task strategies, logic, home/work relationship, time, and involvement. A high score on 'social support' indicates 'you have a well-developed social support system and use supportive relationships to help alleviate the stress you experience'. 'Task strategies' indicates 'you reorganize your work or embark on specific tasks to help cope with the stress you experience'. A high score on the 'logic' scale indicates 'you adopt an unemotional and rational approach to the situations that cause you stress and operate on an objective as opposed to subjective basis'. 'Home/work relationship' coping means 'you use the support you receive from the home environment, hobbies or outside interests to alleviate the effects of stress'. 'Time' means 'you cope with the stress you are experiencing by using time more efficiently perhaps to allow more work to be done in the time available'. And 'involvement' coping suggests that 'you become involved and committed in the issues causing you stress and cope with it by being aware of the reality of the problem'.

Questions 6, 12, 18 and 28 make up the social support coping scale; questions 5, 15, 20, 21, 23, 24 and 27 the task strategy coping scale; questions 8, 10 and 22 the logic coping scale; questions 7, 11, 13 and 17 the home environment as a social support scale; questions 1, 3, 9 and 25 the time coping scale; and finally questions 2, 4, 14, 16, 19 and 26 the involvement coping scale. Add up your scores for each of these scales, and the higher the score the more you use that particular coping strategy.

How You Cope with Stress You Experience

While there are variations in the ways individuals react to sources of pressure and the effects of stress, generally speaking we all make some attempt at coping with these difficulties – consciously or subconsciously. This questionnaire lists a number of potential coping strategies which you are required to rate in terms of the extent to which you actually use them as ways of coping with stress.

Please answer by circling the number of your answer on the scale shown overleaf.

Very extensively used by me   6
Extensively used by me   5
On balance used by me   4
On balance not used by me   3
Seldom used by me   2
Never used by me   1

1 Deal with the problems immediately as they occur   6 5 4 3 2 1
2 Try to recognize my own limitations   6 5 4 3 2 1
3 'Buy time' and stall the issue   6 5 4 3 2 1
4 Look for ways to make the work more interesting   6 5 4 3 2 1
5 Reorganize my work   6 5 4 3 2 1
6 Seek support and advice from my superiors   6 5 4 3 2 1
7 Resort to hobbies and pastimes   6 5 4 3 2 1
8 Try to deal with the situation objectively in an
   unemotional way   6 5 4 3 2 1
9 Effective time management   6 5 4 3 2 1
10 Suppress emotions and try not to let the stress show   6 5 4 3 2 1
11 Having a home that is a 'refuge'   6 5 4 3 2 1
12 Talk to understanding friends   6 5 4 3 2 1
13 Deliberately separate 'home' and 'work'   6 5 4 3 2 1
14 'Stay busy'   6 5 4 3 2 1
15 Plan ahead   6 5 4 3 2 1
16 Not 'bottling things up' and being able to release
   energy   6 5 4 3 2 1
17 Expand interests and activities outside work   6 5 4 3 2 1
18 Have stable relationships   6 5 4 3 2 1
19 Use selective attention (concentrating on specific
   problems)   6 5 4 3 2 1
20 Use distractions (to take your mind off things)   6 5 4 3 2 1
21 Set priorities and deal with problems accordingly   6 5 4 3 2 1
22 Try to 'stand aside' and think through the situation   6 5 4 3 2 1
23 Resort to rules and regulations   6 5 4 3 2 1
24 Delegation   6 5 4 3 2 1
25 Force one's behaviour and lifestyle to slow down   6 5 4 3 2 1
26 Accept the situation and learn to live with it   6 5 4 3 2 1
27 Try to avoid the situation   6 5 4 3 2 1
28 Seek as much social support as possible   6 5 4 3 2 1

**Source: Coping Scale of the Occupational Stress Indicator,
NFER-Nelson, 1988**

The Copers

It is certainly true that our stress survivors are a product of their past, in terms of current experiences and their coping strategies. As John Milton wrote: 'the childhood shows the man, as morning shows the day'. These individuals seem to be able to draw on a range or repertoire of coping strategies that many other people do not have available or do not tend to use. They can draw on both physical and emotional support systems, exercise and relaxation, and can protect themselves and redefine the world around through cognitive reappraisal. They are the modern-day warriors, who meet the challenge with a challenge, choosing from their armoury a range of appropriate weapons. They approach the obstacles of life, not with timidity or circumspection but with a determined response. The stress survivors are by definition the Princes and Princesses of Coping as Machiavelli himself suggested: 'I hold strongly to this; that it is better to be impetuous than circumspect; because fortune is a woman and if she is to be submissive it is necessary to beat and coerce her. Experience shows she is more often subdued by men who do this than by those who act coldly.'

8

Advice to Others

In this chapter we will explore the ways in which people can begin to deal with stressful events, drawing on the coping strategies of our stress survivors. We will attempt to provide the reader with some tips for effective coping, and exercises to help people highlight their idiosyncratic stress profile. Some of this material is drawn from one of the author's books entitled *Living with Stress*, which is a much more comprehensive attempt to deal with the everyday and chronic pressures of life. This chapter is meant only as a beginning, in helping people to learn from our stress survivors, and survive themselves.

Being Positive

Almost all of our stress survivors had one thing in common, they tended to be positive about life, even in times of great despair and confusion. They never gave up hope of overcoming the 'downturn', of knowing that ultimately they had to face up to the situation and cope with it. They were optimists as opposed to pessimists, they saw the opportunities and the 'good side' of harrowing events. As Eddie Shah suggested:

'Everything that has ever happened to me, even the downside, has always ended up as an upside, and that's the important thing. You see, one of the things about life is that a lot of people always look at the downside, they always look at life as if something is going to go wrong. They never say, well, hang on, what's the good side of this, where can I go from here, where's the springboard from here.'

The corollary to this is actually to seek risk, seek achievement as a means of protecting yourself, as Rick Wakeman suggests:

'You're never going to get rid of stress, it's all around you. It's part of you, it lives in your family, it's often caused not by yourself, but by things happening around you. You hang on to your sanity and cope by achieving something. The real way of getting rid of stress is to produce some satisfaction from achieving things, because you can always think, well, I've at least done that. It makes *you* something, at a dinner party, in a pub or even meeting your friends. Someone in the conversation says "Well, we went to Disneyland" and you can say, "Yes, well, I made Mickey Mouse's ears". However stupid or insignificant you think it is [your achievement], if you've achieved something, it is yours and it's a great help.'

Wayne Dyer, author of *Your Erroneous Zones*, feels that people must remain positive, see their achievements and the positive side of their crises and dilemmas. He refers to these behaviours as being 'self mobilized'. Indeed, he believes that individuals must be able to identify their problem areas and patterns of behaving which are negative, and then to 'cut through the lifetime of emotional red tape' by changing their behaviour and redesigning these patterns. What Dyer warns against, and this is a cardinal rule, is blaming any circumstance or other persons for your own failures; in other words, own up and be positive, see the solutions, not the obstacles. This sort of approach to the stresses and strains of life is certainly true of our stress survivors; they are like the people referred to by George Bernard Shaw in *Mrs Warren's Profession*: 'People are always blaming their circumstances for what they are. I don't believe in circumstances. The people who get on in this world are the people who get up and look for the circumstances they want, and if they can't find them, make them.'

Creating Your Own Lifestyle

As well as seeing life in a more positive way, it is also important to adapt your lifestyle to suit your personality. We found it very significant that many of our stress survivors were very much aware of themselves, and what were the positive and negative aspects of their lifestyles. The 'stress resilient' personality has learned to recognize his or her Achilles' heel, and has adapted accordingly. Indeed, some have even created their own stress to stimulate themselves, but then managed that process well.

Derek Jameson is one such resilient or hardy personality:

'The greater the adversity, the greater the problem becomes, the better I cope with it, in a funny sort of way. That's why I said to you at the beginning, can you get hooked on adrenalin, because I thrive on tension and stress. However, when things hot up, I think you've got to keep your cool. The thing that made me successful as a broadcaster and an editor is that I always keep calm, I'm always neutral. I don't get het up, and I don't get confused. I can see my way through to the light at the end of the tunnel, because I know which tunnel I am entering.'

Advice abounds nowadays on how to live your life, what kind of food to eat, what exercise to take or on what particular qualities constitute a 'healthy and creative lifestyle'. For each of us, however, there may be a variety of such lifestyles, but Karl Albrecht, author of *Stress and the Manager*, provides a useful framework for exploring a 'reasonable pattern of living', which many of us might use as a reference point.

Stressful Lifestyle	Low-stress Lifestyle
Individual experiences chronic, unrelieved stress.	Individual accepts 'creative' stress for distinct periods of challenging activity.
Becomes trapped in one or more continuing stressful situations. Struggles with stressful interpersonal relationships (family, spouse, lover, boss, co-workers, etc.).	Has 'escape routes' allowing occasional detachment and relaxation. Asserts own rights and needs; negotiates low-stress relationships of mutual respect; selects friends carefully, and establishes relationships that are nourishing and non-toxic.
Engages in distasteful, dull, toxic, or otherwise unpleasant and unrewarding work.	Engages in challenging, satisfying, worthwhile work that offers intrinsic rewards for accomplishment.
Experiences continual time stress; too much to be done in available time.	Maintains a well-balanced and challenging workload; overloads and crises are balanced by 'breather' periods.

Worries about potentially unpleasant upcoming events.	Balances threatening events with worthwhile goals and positive events to look forward to.
Has poor health habits (e.g., eating, smoking, liquor, lack of exercise, poor level of physical fitness). Life activities are 'lopsided' or unbalanced (e.g., preoccupied with one activity such as work, social activities, making money, solitude or physical activities).	Maintains high level of physical fitness, eats well, uses alcohol and tobacco not at all or sparingly. Life activities are balanced: individual invests energies in a variety of activities, which in the aggregate bring feelings of satisfaction (e.g., work, social activities, recreation, solitude, cultural pursuits, family and close relationships).
Finds it difficult just to 'have a good time', relax and enjoy momentary activities. Experiences sexual activities as unpleasant, unrewarding, or socially 'programmed' (e.g., by manipulation, 'one-upping').	Finds pleasure in simple activities, without feeling a need to justify playful behaviour. Enjoys a full and exuberant sex life, with honest expression of sexual appetite.
Sees life as a serious, difficult situation; little sense of humour.	Enjoys life on the whole; can laugh at himself/herself; has a well-developed and well-exercised sense of humour.
Conforms to imprisoning, punishing social roles.	Lives a relatively role-free life; is able to express natural needs, desires and feelings without apology.
Accepts high-pressure or stressful situations passively; suffers in silence.	Acts assertively to re-engineer pressure situations whenever possible; renegotiates impossible deadlines; avoids placing himself in unnecessary pressure situations; manages time effectively.

Source: Karl Albrecht, *Stress and the Manager*, 1979, pp. 107–8

Belief in Oneself

It was apparent from our stress survivors that, even though many of them suffered from a certain degree of self-doubt, they all had a very well-defined sense of self-worth, or belief in themselves, which helped them to order the reality around them and cope with the stresses and strains of life. The pay-offs are great if you can feel that there is a purpose to your life or behaviour, that you have some talent that differentiates you from others. One must look with some admiration at the clarity of action and purpose which such a sense of mission imparts. No doubt, as the American psychologist George Kelly has suggested, a set of clear 'core constructs' of self are fundamental in providing the individual with clarity of purpose and a strong belief in one's own ability. Petula Clark, the pop singer, once aptly described this in Cooper and Thompson's book *Public Faces, Private Lives*: 'I feel that one has got to be strong in one's self; it's got to be like a steel cord going all the way through, and it's got to be there. You've got to have that invisible courage running through you like steel.'

This belief in oneself can provide the individual with a sense of control, or direction, or security, or a *raison d'être* for their activities, as Elizabeth Emanuel illustrates:

'You've got to have a very big belief in your own talent, because it would be a horrible thing to try and be the best, to try and cope with this whole rat race, if you didn't really feel confident that you can do it. Now, if you really believe you've got something, you've got to believe that you're better than everybody else, then you've got something to give, you really then have something unique to give. This will be your protection and your strength.'

In order for any of us to help to develop a better sense of self-worth, it is important to understand oneself, or as Walt Whitman the poet suggested in this one-liner: 'the whole theory of the universe is directed unerringly to one single individual – namely to you.' The key questions to ask are, 'Who am I?', 'Where am I now?' and 'Where do I want to be?' Psychologists Bill Pfeiffer and John Jones have provided a useful framework for exploring these issues in their life-planning exercise. If you are interested in trying to find out more about yourself, try the following three exercises. The first part is aimed at answering the question 'Where am I now?' in three areas – your career, your personal life (friends and family) and your personal fulfilment, and it proceeds as follows:

1. Draw a graph or life-line, which can be straight or curved, that depicts the trend of the past, present and future of your career. Place an X to show where you are now. Then write a brief explanation of the career line you have drawn, highlighting the high points and the low points.
2. Repeat the procedure to create a life-line for your personal life with highs and lows.
3. Repeat again to create a personal fulfilment life-line.

This part of the exercise should give you some idea of where you've been, where you are now and where you are likely to go. The future aspects of each line may reflect either your hopes for where you *ideally* would go or where you think you are likely to end up (although you would rather not).

The second part of the exercise asks you to find out 'Who am I?', by writing down up to twenty career adjectives which most accurately describe you in your work, such as ambitious, trustworthy, nonchalant, and so on. Then write down a similar list of adjectives for your personal life and personal fulfilment. Divide each group of adjectives into three categories: positive, negative and neutral. This regrouping can provide you with an awareness of your positive and negative traits in three major aspects of your life.

In the third part of the exercise, ask yourself where you want to be. List up to ten ideal attainments in each of the three main life areas – career, personal life and personal fulfilment. Goals might include 'I want to become self-employed', or 'I want to re-establish closeness with my husband', or 'I want to face my need for alcohol'. Then assign priority values to the ideals within each of the three groups, using the following scale: 4 = of very great importance; 3 = of great importance; 2 = of moderate importance; and 1 = of little importance. Finally, combine all the ideals into one group and rank them again, using the same scoring system. The combined list should reflect the relative importance of specific goals, whether they involve your career, personal life or personal fulfilment. This then gives you information about your 'ideal' goals in life. You are now equipped with a launching pad for life planning.

A way to begin your planning efforts would be to select five or so of the highest rated goals and establish a programme to achieve them, one by one. You will need to think out the behavioural, emotional and practical strategies for each goal. Such an effort is not easy, but by writing out your goals and strategies you may see solutions you had not conceived before.

Relaxation Exercise

As we can see from the last chapter, many of our stress survivors took time out to relax, to unwind during a busy day or week. For many of us who have hectic lifestyles and feel overloaded, it is important to make an effort during the day to put aside some time to reflect, to rest, to experience solitude. Meditation and relaxation exercises have been found to help reduce fatigue, control blood pressure and generally make an individual feel psychologically better.

Transcendental meditation (TM), for example, has been reported to help work adjustment through the reduction of tension. Meditation involves concentration on a single stimulus, which is repeated twice a day for approximately twenty minutes. The object of this technique is to restrict one's mental and physical states – the end result being a tranquil mind–body state. The effects of anxiety are kept to a minimum during this period of sustained concentration on a solitary object or word – a mantra. A number of researchers have found that TM can subsequently improve performance, reduce short-term anxiety reactions, and increase span of attention. It has been argued by some psychologists that TM is most effective in breaking the threat–arousal–threat spiral, so that after the individual has experienced a stressful event he/she can relax. TM and other relaxation techniques can, therefore, in the short term, help the individual to prepare his/her bodily processes for the stresses and pressures of everyday life.

Aside from the traditional TM, one can use a whole range of relaxation techniques. For example, Herbert Benson of Harvard suggests the following technique:

1. Sit quietly in a comfortable position.
2. Close your eyes.
3. Beginning at your feet and progressing up to your face, deeply relax your muscles. Keep them relaxed.
4. Breathe through your nose. Become aware of your breathing. As you breathe out, say the word *one* silently to yourself. Continue the pattern; breathe in . . . out, *one*; in . . . out, *one*; and so on. Breathe easily and naturally.
5. Continue for ten to twenty minutes. You may open your eyes to check the time, but do not use an alarm. When you finish, sit quietly for several minutes, first with your eyes closed and later with your eyes open. Do not stand up for a few minutes.
6. Do not worry about whether you are successful in achieving a deep level of relaxation. Maintain a passive attitude and permit relaxation to occur at its own pace. When distracting thoughts occur, try to ignore them by not dwelling on them and return to repeating *one*. With practice, the response should come with little effort. Practise the technique once or twice daily but not within two hours of any meal, since the digestive processes seem to interfere with eliciting the relaxation response.

Social Support

As we have been able to see in this book, each of our stress survivors meets the world and copes with its pressures with a complex set of emotional characteristics, coping styles, values and attitudes. Despite the importance of this individual make-up and the repertoire of one's coping strategies, many studies have shown that a positive and nurturing support group, such as the family, friends and co-workers, can offset many of the nefarious effects of stress. Eddie Shah has certainly been helped by his wife and business partner during his turbulent career:

'A few people have influenced me more than anything else in my life. One is Jennifer, my wife, and the other is Helen, my business partner. Jennifer has been my main support in life generally. Helen has also influenced me tremendously, because she is my other support. She is the one that when I go off "down track" at work, she will always pull me back. But at the end of the day, if she really feels I want to do something, she'll go with me, even though she disagrees with me. She'll make it work. And she's a very, very able woman, and therefore she looks after the business much better than I do, and turns it round and makes things happen. So I think these two people have had more effect on me than anybody else.'

Social support and maintaining a close relationship is also essential in a marriage, as Nina Carter has found from her experience:

'I think it is essential to spend as much time as you can together to discuss your everyday lives, to talk about your jobs and to take part and an interest in each other. It is important to make sure, particularly when you have children, that you always allow enough time to be together, because it is a known fact your children grow up and leave home at some point, and then you are left alone together. If you've got nothing to say to each other, then that's a tragic end to the partnership. So, I think it's important to keep a "team spirit" feeling in a marriage. You have to try as hard as you can, no matter how difficult it is, and it is difficult, particularly when you have children because they are so demanding.'

Joanna Foster agrees and claims that we need support in all aspects of our lives from time to time:

'The family and the marriage is a vital social support system. I believe it is crucial for couples to have constant dialogue, from very early in their relationship. Sometimes people need professional support as well. You know, I'm still very struck about how very suspicious people are about getting any professional counselling or therapy, but people who need help in their relationships or in stress generally, should use marriage guidance or Relate or counsellors or whatever it is, rather than have to struggle by themselves, which they are very often ill equipped to do. In coping with the pressures of life, seeking support and sorting out support systems I would put very high on the agenda.'

Even in the workplace, the advice from our stress survivors is seek people you like and feel would support you and others at work, as Sir Terence Conran highlights: 'I suppose the most important advice I can give is to do things that you really enjoy doing, for if you really enjoy doing them, it won't seem like work. And, most importantly, surround yourself with people that you like and get on with, and don't simply get people into your business that you have little regard for.'

It is clear that a husband or wife and the immediate family can be a major source of support. They provide the problem-solving, listening and acceptance that can relieve stress even though they may not be able to solve the related problems. One study of 190 engineers, accountants and their wives showed that the more compatible the husbands and wives were, the higher the likelihood that the men could cope better with stress-related problems at work and home. Studies of Norwegian prisoners of war in Nazi concentration camps showed that close social support was essential to their survival. Individuals who had been able to retain close ties with family, friends and religious or political groups survived more often, and were best able to adjust to normal life when freed.

Looking at Life Differently

Relaxing, exercising, changing your lifestyle and seeking social support are all aimed at building your 'stress resiliency', and lowering your reactions to stressful events, individuals and situations. The following section will examine ways of lowering your overall reactions to stressful events by managing your perceptions of daily events. As we discussed in earlier chapters, the way an individual perceives a situation dramatically affects the stress response experienced. For example, Type A individuals continually set off their stress responses by perceiving life as competitive, achievement-orientated and time-driven. People who have an 'external' locus of control perceive that they have little control over the situations which confront them.

In contrast, the 'hardy personality' perceives he/she has a great deal of control over his/her life. In the last two cases, it is not so much the actual ability to cope with a situation, but the individual's perception of his/her ability to cope that matters. Many of our stress survivors were able to look at events very differently, to take a much more positive approach.

There are a range of techniques available to help people reappraise or perceive many stressful situations in a more positive light. One such technique was developed by Jim and Jonathan Quick in their book *Organizational Stress and Preventive Management*. They describe what they call 'constructive self-talk', or the 'mental monologue' that most people conduct about the events they experience and their reactions to these events. This monologue or 'self-talk' can range from being gently positive to harshly condemning. When people engage in 'negative self-talk', they achieve nothing; they simply maintain the stress and dissipate their emotional energy. If you are involved in 'constructive self-talk', it can achieve more positive psychological results. For example, for someone recovering from a heart attack, he/she is likely to have the following mental monologue, 'I almost died, I may die soon. I'll never be able to work again.' Instead, they could engage in constructive 'self-talk', such as, 'I didn't die, I made it through. And the doctor says I'll be able to get back to work soon.'

Another technique one could use is what Karl Albrecht refers to as 'quick recovery', that is, the ability to bounce back from upsetting experiences. We have seen in the last chapter many examples of this among our stress survivors. Learning to recover quickly takes little more than an awareness of how you actually do recover. As Albrecht describes it: 'Once you begin to think about your emotional responses, you can recognize the process of returning to emotional equilibrium after a provocation has passed.' For example, if you find yourself drawn into a personal confrontation, you are likely to experience anger and a full-blown stress response. 'Your higher level mental processes will probably not be functioning very well,' Albrecht explains. 'However, at a certain point, your emotions will begin to subside and you will realize that you are angry. That is, you will experience your anger as an intellectual concept as well as a physical feeling.' Albrecht states that at this point you have the option to continue and aggravate your angry feelings by 'rehashing the provocation, rejustifying your position, reopening a new attack on your adversaries, and becoming newly outraged by their unreasonable behaviour'. A quick recovery approach would suggest you stop this 'negative circular' approach, become more rational and less conscious of your need to 'win'.

Gaining Control

We have seen from our stress survivors that when they felt in control, they tended to overcome their stress more easily. One way of gaining control is to learn to become more assertive. Assertiveness is not about being aggressive or establishing your rights or behaviour over someone else. As Alberti and Emmons in their book *Your Perfect Right: A Guide to Assertive Behavior* suggest, the assertive person is 'open and flexible, genuinely concerned with the rights of others', yet at the same time 'able to establish very well his or her own rights'. Psychologist Sandra Langrish illustrates this definition by highlighting the differences between non-assertive, aggressive and assertive behaviour:

Imagine, for example, you are working on a project. It is 4.30 p.m. and you have arranged to meet a friend at 5.00 p.m., so that you can go for a meal and a theatre visit together. Your boss rushes into your office waving a piece of paper. He has just received a telephone call about some aspect of the project which requires the preparation of an additional document, ' . . . right now!' You realize it will take until at least 6.45 to do the work. What do you say?
Non-assertive Response: 'That's OK. I'll drop what I'm doing and do it right now. Just leave it with me. I'll take care of it.'
Aggressive Response: 'What do you take me for! Do you think I've got nothing better to do than jump when you whistle? Well, if you do, you've got a big shock coming! I'm going out with a friend, and I'm leaving at 5.00 on the dot. Just find someone else to run after you.'
Assertive Response: 'I realize that it's important that this is done as soon as possible, but I've made arrangements to meet a friend at 5.00 p.m., so I can't do it now. However, I'll do it first thing tomorrow.'

Increasingly, training and self-help programmes are being established to help people become more assertive. These programmes usually involve several stages. First, a self-assessment of 'under what circumstances' and 'with what people' individuals find it difficult to assert themselves. Second, to identify particular circumstances that can be improved. Third, to practise more assertive behaviour in similar or simulated situations through role-playing. Assertiveness training also tends to teach individuals how to deal with situations likely to overcome their natural assertive behaviour. Galassi and Galassi in their book *Assert Yourself*, and Sandra Langrish in *Improving Interpersonal Relations*, suggest a number of personal skills needed to enhance assertiveness. These skills are of two kinds, verbal and non-verbal:

Broken Record: a skill that by calm repetition, saying what you want over and over again, teaches persistence, and permits you to ignore manipulative verbal side traps, argumentative baiting and irrelevant logic, while sticking to your desired point. This is particularly effective with persistent salesmen.

Fogging: a skill that teaches the acceptance of manipulative criticism by calmly acknowledging to your critic the probability that there may be some truth in what he or she says, yet allows you to remain your own judge of what you do. It allows you to receive criticism comfortably without becoming anxious or defensive.

Negative Assertion: a skill that teaches acceptance of your errors and faults (without having to apologize), by strongly and sympathetically agreeing with hostile or constructive criticism of your negative qualities. It permits you to look more comfortably at negative elements in your own behaviour without feeling defensive and anxious, or resorting to denial of real errors.

Negative Inquiry: a skill that teaches the active prompting of criticism in order to use the information (if helpful) or exhaust it (if manipulative), while prompting your critic to be more assertive and less dependent on manipulative ploys. It encourages the other person to express honest negative feelings and improves communication.

Workable Compromise: a skill to use whenever you feel your self-respect is not in question. Here, you offer a workable compromise to the other person. However, if the end goal involves a matter of your self-worth, there can be no compromise.

Keeping in mind the difference between aggressiveness and assertiveness, many individuals would benefit from assertiveness training. The goal of assertiveness training is to help people to learn to solve problems and enable them to say, 'I feel OK about myself. I don't have to make others feel not OK in order for me to get my needs met. I know what I want. I feel good about myself and others. I can think and I have confidence to ask for what I want.'

Managing Your 'Hurry Sickness'

Many of our stress survivors were able to lead perfectly normal Type A lives by managing or controlling their natural enthusiasm for total work involvement, or what Meyer Friedman and Ray Rosenman term 'hurry sickness'. In their book, *Type A Behavior and Your Heart*, cardiologists Friedman and Rosenman recommend a number of 'drills against hurry sickness', for people wanting to prevent heart disease or any other type of stress-related illness, and to manage their Type A lifestyle. Many of their suggestions may appear to be humorous or flippant, given the seriousness of stress-induced diseases, but the authors feel that one's total lifestyle must be systematically managed to prevent the excesses of Type A behaviour:

1. Try to restrain yourself from being the centre of attention by constantly talking. Force yourself to listen to others. 'Begin in your advocational hours to listen quietly to the conversation of other people. Quit trying to finish their sentences. An even better sort of drill for you if you have been in the habit of hastening the other person's speech rhythms is to seek out a person who stutters and then deliberately remain tranquil.' If you continue to need to talk unnecessarily, perhaps you ought to ask yourself the following questions: (1) Do I really have anything important to say? (2) Does anyone want to hear it? and (3) Is this the time to say it?
2. Try and be patient in all aspects of your life. Try the following drill: 'Purposely, with a companion, frequent restaurants and theatres where you know there will be a period

of waiting. If your companion is your wife, remember that you spend far longer periods of time alone with her in your own home without fidgeting. If you and your companion cannot find enough to say to each other as you wait in a restaurant or a theatre, then you had both better seek different companions.'

3. Try to control your obsessional time-directed life by making yourself aware of it and changing the established pattern of behaviour. For example, 'whenever you catch yourself speeding up your car in order to get through a yellow light at an intersection, penalize yourself by immediately turning to the right (or left) at the next corner. Circle the block and approach the same corner and signal light again. After such penalization you may find yourself racing a yellow light a second, but probably not a third time.'

4. Develop reflective periods in your self-created 'hectic programme for life', creating opportunities to assess the causes of your hurry sickness. One of the most important new habits to develop is a weekly review of the original causes of your present hurry sickness. Try to get to the source of your problems and current obsessions. Is your time-dominated behaviour really a need to feel important? Is it designed to avoid some activity or person? Is it really essential to the success of a particular goal? Friedman and Rosenman offer this advice: 'Never forget when confronted by any task to ask yourself the following questions: (1) will this matter have importance five years from now? and (2) must I do this right now, or do I have enough time to think about the best way to accomplish it?'

5. As part of an effort to broaden yourself and lessen specific aspects of obsessional time-dictated behaviour, indulge in some outside activities: theatre, reading, sewing, and so on. Friedman and Rosenman recommend that patients 'for drill purposes, attempt to read books that demand not only your entire attention but also a certain amount of patience. We have repeatedly advised our Type A patients to attempt reading Proust's eight-volume novel *The Remembrance of Things Past* not because it is one of the great modern classics (which it is) but because the author needs several chapters to

describe an event that most Type A subjects would have handled in a sentence or two.'

6. Try not to make unnecessary appointments or deadlines. 'Remember, the more unnecessary deadlines you make for yourself, the worse your "hurry sickness" becomes.'

7. Learn to protect your time and to say No. 'Try to never forget that if you fail to protect your allotment of time, no one else will. And the older you become, the more important this truth is.'

8. Take as many 'stress-free breathing spaces' during the course of an intensive working day as possible. 'Learn to interrupt long or even short sessions of any type of activity that you know or suspect may induce tension and stress before it is finished. Such stress is particularly apt to rise in the course of writing long memos, reports or articles.' Taking the pressure off your stressful task – by reading the newspaper or taking a brief stretch – is the kind of behaviour suggested here.

9. Try to create opportunities during the day or night when you can totally relax your body and mind.

Expressing Your Emotions

Many of our stress survivors indicated that they were able to express their emotions in times of crisis, either by crying, expressing anger or venting their hostility. There were some who, under extreme conditions, found it difficult to do so, for example, Stuart Hall after the death of his son. As Stuart Hall indicated, by burying his emotions he made things worse for his wife and himself. It was only when he was able to express them that things began to change for the better. So, in addition to taking advantage of the physical outlet provided by exercise and relaxation, you may also find stress relief through talking or writing about your feelings. Talking about your feelings to an understanding friend, colleague or relative is one of the most common and effective ways of dealing with grief or disappointment or rejection. If you find it difficult to discuss it with a person on a face-to-face basis at the beginning, then it might be useful to write down your thoughts, feelings and concerns.

Keeping a regular diary or journal of your feelings, or simply dashing off an angry letter that is either thrown away or later revised when emotions have cooled, can be therapeutic.

Some people have found that maintaining a stress diary can be helpful. It allows you to identify the activities and individuals that cause you the most difficulty. An awareness, on a daily or weekly time frame, during a period of stress, can help you to develop an 'action plan' to minimize or eliminate the stress factor, or, at the very least, alert you to when a stressful event is about to take place. This diary could be kept on a daily or weekly or incident basis. When a crisis incident or series of events occur, just jot them down, describing the incident, the people involved, what you did and what you should have done. This should help you to express your feelings, as well as see how you can best deal with this type of situation in the future. Each incident and/or relationship may be better managed in the future if you accurately identify the problem and systematically think through the options or alternative methods of coping.

If you have recognized a need to deal with stress in your life, you have taken the first important step towards successfully dealing with the problem. This vital *recognition*, however important, must be matched equally with *determination* and *patience*. It is the determination to face truths about yourself and make necessary changes that will provide staying power when the going gets rough, as our stress survivors have illustrated throughout this book. In addition, you must have the patience to understand that change does not come about quickly; personal change and growth are both gradual processes.

Conclusion: The Stress Survivor Profile

What, besides their success, marks our stress survivors as being in some way different from others who may not have coped so well? Can we account for this extra ingredient, this set of experiences and coping facets which make them exceptional? From our interviews, we found a number of general patterns which, although they did not apply to everyone, occurred with startling regularity among our group. These form a kind of generic profile of the 'stress survivor' in the public eye, and might serve as a lesson for us all.

Learning from Childhood

We believe that early childhood experiences played a significant part in moulding the attitudes, behaviour and coping strategies of our stress survivors. For some of our group, childhood was in the psychological sense a traumatic period of insecurity, and in some cases loss. These events provided some with the drive and need to control their own future. For others, a particular parent provided the role model (in both a negative and positive way) or platform for their later approaches to coping with life. What was critical about their early life experiences was that all of them were obviously very much aware of these early events, learned from them and adapted their behaviour to cope with the exigencies of their later life.

Resilient Personality Types

Although our stress survivors displayed a range of personality characteristics, from Type A behavioural patterns to 'internals' (in terms of control), to high achievers, they were above all 'resilient' or hardy personality types. They demonstrated in their behaviour a positive approach to life, seeing obstacles as challenges, commitments as growth and pessimism as an ana-thema. They were the eternal optimists and adaptable copers, even under enormous adversity.

Pathfinders

In Gail Sheehy's terms, these stress survivors were 'path-finders'. They successfully navigated the dangerous 'waters of life' with determination, commitment, energy and adaptability, which not only prevented them from sinking but also chan-nelled them through positive and calmer waters. There were the occasional monsoons or tidal waves, but they seemed to transcend them, internalizing the experience for the next climactic encounter.

Victims of Spill-over – Learning from the Past

Although our stress survivors were able to cope with most

things, they had great difficulty in coping with the intrusion of their professional lives into their private lives. The spill-over effect of work was extremely pronounced for this group, and although a number of them 'lost relationships' along the way, they all were aware of this and were attempting to develop coping strategies to deal with this in the future. The primary coping approach was to shore up the supportive nature of their personal relationships – the family was certainly high on the agenda, but sometimes very difficult to sustain.

Seeking Control

Most of our group were driven to regain or exercise control over their own destiny, to achieve a position where they, rather than events, dictated their future. In attempting to gain control, many were able to learn from their failures and negative experiences.

Redefinition of Their World

Many of the stress survivors were extremely good at redefining negative events, seeing them as positive, or cognitively re-appraising them in a way that made them less destructive or damaging, and more easily resolvable. They are individuals who approach the obstacles of life not with timidity or caution but with a positive and determined response.

Support Seekers

In addition to possessing extremely good skills at communicating and allowing themselves to be open and honest about their feelings and attitudes, they are unafraid to seek support when they need it. Although many of them are self-reliant types, they are also capable of knowing when, and from whom, support should be sought.

It seems as if the lessons we can learn from our stress survivors are to experience and embrace life, learn from it, reflect on its purpose and structure our values accordingly. It is ironic that after several decades of research into stress, coping and its effect on health, that a lay psychologist of the 1930s, Wilfrid Northfield, should have written in his simple book on *Curing*

Nervous Tension a recipe for coping with stress that best sums up the philosophy of many of our stress survivors:

A great many people, I believe, take their work too seriously. It is good to be keen and conscientious, but to be over-sensitive places a great strain upon the nervous system. If you do your best, you cannot do more. To lie awake at night and think about some paltry error you made during the day is the height of folly. There is not a human being who has not made a mistake at some time or other. Try to get a correct sense of values. A small human error can be easily adjusted, should you accidentally make one. But your nervous system, your soul, cannot be so easily repaired. So guard it and preserve it by taking your duties light-heartedly, without sacrificing your zeal and efficiency.

References

Alberti, R.D. and Emmons, M.L. (1970) *Your Perfect Right: A Guide to Assertive Behavior*. New York: Impact.

Albrecht, K. (1979) *Stress and the Manager. Making it Work for You*. New Jersey: Prentice-Hall.

Barnard, C.J. (1948) *The Function of the Executive*. Boston: Harvard University Press.

Benson, H. et al. (1973) 'Decreased Systolic Blood Pressure in Hypertensive Subjects Who Practiced Meditation', *Journal of Clinical Investigation*, 52.

Bortner, R.W. (1969) 'A Short Rating Scale as a Potential Measure of Pattern A Behavior', *Journal of Chronic Diseases*, 22, 87–91.

Carruthers, M.E. (1976) 'Risk Factor Control', conference paper entitled 'Stress of Air Traffic Control Officers', Manchester, April.

Conran, S. (1977) *Superwoman*. Harmondsworth: Penguin.

Cooper, C.L. (1981) *Improving Interpersonal Relations*. Hampshire: Gower Press.

Cooper, C.L. and Hingley, P. (1985) *The Change Makers*. London: Harper & Row.

Cooper, C.L. and Thompson, L. (1984) *Public Faces, Private Lives*. London: Fontana.

Cooper, C.L., Cooper, R.D. and Eaker, L.H. (1988) *Living with Stress*. Harmondsworth: Penguin.

Cooper, C.L., Sloan, S. and Williams, S. (1979) *Occupational Stress Indicator*. Windsor: NFER-Nelson.

Cox, C. and Cooper, C.L. (1988) *High Flyers*. Oxford: Basil Blackwell.

Cox, C.M. (1926) *The Early Mental Traits of Three Hundred Geniuses*. California: Stanford University Press.

Cummings, T. and Cooper, C.L. (1979) 'A Cybernetic Framework for the Study of Occupational Stress', *Human Relations*, 32, 395–439.

Davidson, M.J. and Cooper, C.L. (1983) *Stress and the Woman Manager*. Oxford: Blackwell.

Davidson, M.J. and Cooper, C.L. (eds) (1987) *Women and Information Technology*. Chichester: John Wiley.

Dyer, W.W. (1976) *Your Erroneous Zones*. New York: Avon Books.

Evans, P. and Bartolomé, F. (1980) *Must Success Cost So Much?* London: Grant McIntyre.

Friday, N. (1977) *My Mother, My Self*. London: Fontana.

Friedman, M.D. and Rosenman, R.H. (1974) *Type A Behavior and Your Heart*. New York: Knopf.

Galassi, M.D. and Galassi, J.P. (1977) *Assert Yourself: How to be Your Own Person*. New York: Human Sciences Press.

Galton, R. (1869) *Hereditary Genius*. London: Macmillan.

Garfield, C. (1986) *Peak Performers*. London: Hutchinson.

Havelock Ellis, Henry (1904) *A Study of British Genius*. London: Hurst and Blackett.

Heller, J. (1975) *Something Happened*. New York: Ballantine.

Hilgard, E.R. et al. (1971) *Introduction to Psychology*. New York: Harcourt Brace Jovanovich.

Kelley, G. (1955) *The Psychology of Personal Constructs*. New York: Norton.

Kobasa, S. (1979) 'Stressful Life Events, Personality, Health: an Enquiry into Hardiness', *Journal of Social Personality*, 37.

Kuna, D.J. (1975) 'Meditation and Work', *Vocation Guidance Quarterly*, 23 (4).

Langrish, S. (1981) 'Assertiveness Training', in C.L. Cooper (ed.), *Improving Interpersonal Relations*. Epping: Gower Press.

Lazarus, R.S. (1976) *Patterns of Adjustment*. New York: McGraw-Hill.

Lewis, S. and Cooper, C.L. (1989) *Career Couples*. London: Unwin Hyman.

Lodge, D. (1989) *Nice Work*. Harmondsworth: Penguin.

Melhuish, A. (1978) *Executive Health*. London: Business Books.

Mettlin, C. (1976) 'Occupational Careers and the Prevention of Coronary Prone Behaviour', *Social Science and Medicine*, 10, 367–72.

Pfeiffer, J.W. and Jones, J.E. (1970) *Structural Experiences for Human Relations Training*. Iowa City: University Associates Press.

Pincherle, A. (1972) 'Fitness for Work', *Proceedings of the Royal Society of Medicine*, 65, 321–4.

Quick, J.C. and Quick, J.D. (1984) *Organizational Stress and Preventive Management*. New York: McGraw-Hill.

Santrock, J.W. (1988) *Children*. Iowa: Brown Publisher.

Scase, R. and Goffee, R. (1989) *Reluctant Managers – Their Work and Life Style*. London: Unwin Hyman.

Selye, H. (1946) 'The General Adaptation Syndrome and the Diseases of Adaptation', *Journal of Clinical Endocrinology*, 6, 117.

Shaffer, M. (1983) *Life After Stress*. Chicago: Contemporary Books.

Sheehy, G. (1976) *Passages: Predictable Crises of Adult Life*. New York: Dutton.

Sheehy, G. (1982) *Pathfinders*. London: Bantam Books.

Tead, O. (1935) *The Art of Leadership*. New York: McGraw-Hill.

Wardwell, W., Hyman, I.M. and Bahnson, C. B. (1964) 'Stress and Coronary Disease in Three Field Studies', *Journal of Chronic Disease*, 17, 73–4.

Zigler, E.F. and Finn-Stevenson, M. (1987) *Children – Development and Social Issues*. Massachusetts: Lexington Books.

Index